Jack London

An American Original

Jack London

An American Original

Rebecca Stefoff

For Zachary, another California-born adventurer

OXFORD
UNIVERSITY PRESS

Oxford New York
Auckland Bangkok Buenos Aires Cape Town Chennai
Dar es Salaam Delhi Hong Kong Istanbul Karachi Kolkata
Kuala Lumpur Madrid Melbourne Mexico City Mumbai Nairobi
São Paulo Shanghai Singapore Taipei Tokyo Toronto
and an associated company in Berlin

Published by Oxford University Press, Inc.
198 Madison Avenue, New York, New York 10016
www.oup.com

Design: Greg Wozney
Layout: Alexis Siroc
Picture Research: Sara Ogger

Library of Congress Cataloging-in-Publication Data

Stefoff, Rebecca, 1951-
Jack London / Rebecca Stefoff.
p. cm. -- (Oxford portraits)
Includes bibliographical references (p.) and index.
Summary: Examines the life, beliefs, adventures, and works of Jack London, American author best known for his tales of hardship and survival set in the Yukon Territory.
ISBN 0-19-512223-2
1. London, Jack, 1876-1916--Juvenile literature. 2. Authors, American--20th century--Biography--Juvenile literature. [1. London, Jack, 1876-1916. 2. Authors, American.] I. Title. II. Series.

PS3523.O46 Z897 2002
813'.52--dc21
[B] 2001053087

987654321

Printed in the United States of America on acid-free paper

On the cover: Jack London aboard his boat the *Roamer* in 1914, photographed by Charmian London
Frontispiece: Jack London at the desk where he wrote some of his adventurous tales

Contents

Jack London in 1895, during his year of high school. He startled some of his fellow students—and his principal—with an essay published in the school paper that concluded, "Arise, ye Americans, patriots and optimists! Awake! Seize the reins of a corrupted government and educate your masses!"

CHAPTER

1

IN THE PUBLIC EYE

On February 10, 1897, a young man stepped onto a soapbox in City Hall Park in downtown Oakland, California, hoping to get arrested.

He was a striking figure. A friend later described him as he looked at about the time of that day in the park: "Sunshine—the word leaps of itself to the end of my pen.... He had a curly mop of hair which seemed spun of gold; his strong neck, with a loose, low soft shirt, was bronzed with it; and his eyes were like a sunlit sea. His clothes were floppy and careless... he was a strange combination of Scandinavian sailor and Greek god, made altogether boyish and lovable by the lack of two front teeth, lost cheerfully somewhere in a fight." That was Jack London at 20.

Atop the soapbox in the park, with supporters and curious onlookers gathered around, he began to speak, using the loud voice and dramatic expressions of a skilled orator to grab the attention of passersby and draw a crowd. Jack London was not a nervous, tongue-tied novice at public speaking. He had been making speeches in that park for more than a year, criticizing a social and economic system that he believed doomed many people to lives of hopelessness and poverty, and singing the praises of the economic philosophy known as socialism, which he felt offered a fairer distribution of wealth and power. He had even made news in San Francisco, Oakland's larger neighbor across the San Francisco Bay. On February 16 of the previous year, an article in the *San Francisco Chronicle* had said: "Jack London, who is known as the boy socialist in Oakland, is holding forth nightly to crowds that throng City Hall Park. There are other speakers in plenty, but London always gets the biggest crowd and the most respectful attention."

Now, a year later, London was expecting more than respectful attention. His fellow socialists in Oakland, as well as some orators who spoke in the park on other topics, were unhappy with an Oakland city law that made it illegal for anyone to conduct a public meeting on a public street without written permission from the mayor. Feeling that this law conflicted with the rights of free speech and free assembly guaranteed by the U. S. Constitution, the speakers had decided that one of them should get arrested and demand a jury trial, which would call attention to how Oakland was abusing their rights. Jack London volunteered to challenge the law. He was the right socialist for the job—not only did he believe the law was unjust, he also enjoyed being in the limelight.

Soon, as usual, a crowd gathered around London, and the police were not far behind. When London refused to end his speech, the police arrested him and took him to jail. Instead of simply paying a fine or spending time in jail, London demanded trial by jury. He acted as his own defense lawyer at the trial, which took place in the City of Oakland Police Court a week later. His argument in favor of free speech was so convincing that all but one of the jurors declared him "not guilty." The city dropped the case, but not before it had been the subject of a flurry of newspaper articles that London's socialist friends regarded as good publicity. They tried to take advantage of that publicity by making London their candidate for a position on the Oakland School Board.

London did not run for the school board, but he had had a few days of celebrity, days during which the spotlight of publicity singled him out as someone special. It was not the only time he would find himself in the public eye. In years to come that spotlight would shine often and long on Jack London, the famous writer. Sometimes, in fact, it would be a little too bright and too hot.

Few writers of the early 20th century were more popular than Jack London, or more controversial. His personality and his work both made strong impressions on all who encountered them. People either loved London and his writing or scorned them—there was no middle ground. Even after he died he continued to arouse strong feelings. In the decades following London's death, literary critics dismissed much of his work as crude and primitive. Many scholars came to regard London, once viewed as one of the leading literary voices of his day, as a minor writer of little lasting importance.

At the same time, however, some of his best and most beloved books and stories, many of them dealing with life in the Far North, quietly became classics. Novels such as *The Call of the Wild* and stories such as "To Build a Fire" continued to captivate readers who were not interested in what the critics thought. Teachers recognized the merits of London's work and introduced generations of students to his storytelling, his powerful explorations of human nature, and his simple, direct, and vigorous use of language. In time, literary critics took a second look at Jack London, the writer whose books simply would not die, and they saw that his best work was an important and distinctively American contribution to the great literature of the world.

Like his writing, London's life drew harsh criticism as well as warm admiration both during his lifetime and afterward. His critics focused on Jack's battles with alcohol, his unsuccessful first marriage, and the rumors of suicide that surrounded his death. Often painting him in an unfairly negative light, they questioned the originality of his ideas and the accuracy of some of his claims. London's political ideas also aroused argument. People opposed to socialism, a philosophy that mainstream America has never embraced, rejected London because of his beliefs—while those who favored socialism complained that he wasn't *enough* of a socialist.

People who knew, loved, or admired London, on the other hand, praised his genius, his generosity, his spirited approach to life, and the drive and determination that lifted him from the gutter to the pinnacle of success and fame. Even today, generations after his death, Jack London attracts earnest defenders and champions, some of whom prefer to ignore or gloss over aspects of his life that they fear might tarnish his image. In reality, London was a complex person, neither purely devilish nor entirely saintly, but, like most people, a combination of both qualities. But nearly everyone who knew him well insisted that there was something special about him, an intense eagerness that made him stand out in any crowd. So vivid and passionate was London's character that those who read his words and study his life can begin to feel that they almost know him.

One reason that London's readers feel they know the writer is that his writing and his life were as closely intertwined as any author's have ever been. Many of his best-known and strongest works draw heavily on his own life story; some of these works are almost autobiographical. However, one cannot simply take London's writing as an accurate record of his life. In order to make a point or tell a more powerful story, he often exaggerated things or added fictional elements to writing that was mostly autobiographical. We cannot always untangle the threads of "real life" and "storytelling" that London wove together so well.

Many writers have drawn on their own lives for subject matter, but London's was an extraordinary life, a mere 40 years crammed with several lifetimes' worth of activity and adventure. In a series of transformations that began when he was a teenager, he became a pirate, a patrolman, a sailor, a hobo, a student, a gold prospector, a journalist and war correspondent, a sought-after public speaker, a yachtsman, and a world traveler. He also became a best-selling author of novels, short stories, articles and essays, plays, and books of social criticism, publishing more than 50 books in a 17-year period. All his adventures and successes came about because at an early age he rebelled against the life that fate seemed to have in store for him—the brutish life of a poor, uneducated, unskilled "work-beast," as he called it.

Jack London's life was so eventful and so colorful that it is easy to imagine that he lived it with his future biographers in mind, wanting to leave a good story for them to tell. In a way, he did. London was very much aware that the legend that grew up about him during his lifetime—a legend rooted in his colorful public personality and the stories he told about his adventures—helped sell his books and pack his lectures with eager listeners. He undoubtedly believed that people would continue talking and writing about him long after his death. Some have said that London's life was his best creation. Perhaps so—but although it was a life lived deliberately in the public eye, it was a genuine life, never a pose. It fulfilled the fiery words that he penned as his own motto:

> I would rather be ashes than dust!
>
> I would rather that my spark should burn out in a brilliant blaze than that it should be stifled by dry rot.
>
> I would rather be a superb meteor, every atom of me in magnificent glow, than a sleepy and permanent planet.
>
> The proper function of man is to live, not to exist.
>
> I shall not waste my days in trying to prolong them.
>
> I shall use my time.

Jack London's time began on January 12, 1876, in San Francisco. His mother, Flora Wellman Chaney, gave birth to her first child in the home of a friend. She had been abandoned by William Henry Chaney, who may or may not have been her husband but who was almost certainly the father of the boy whom Flora named John Griffith Chaney. The sorry tale of his parents is the first mystery in the life of the child who became Jack London, a mystery that Jack never solved entirely.

Jack's mother was born Flora Wellman in 1843 in Massillon, Ohio. As the daughter of a wealthy businessman, she enjoyed a comfortable, even pampered, childhood until she became ill with typhoid fever. Although she recovered, the fever permanently stunted her growth, thinned her hair, and weakened her eyesight. It may also have damaged her mental well being. Later in life she suffered from mood swings and other emotional disturbances, and her son was to find her a difficult and demanding mother. At the age of 20, Wellman left her family and made her way to the West

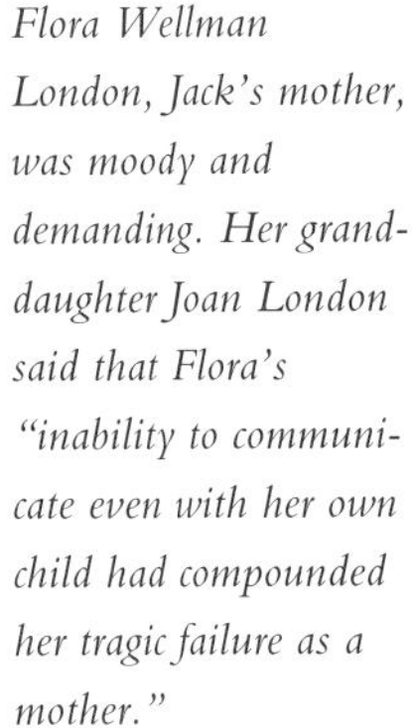

Flora Wellman London, Jack's mother, was moody and demanding. Her granddaughter Joan London said that Flora's "inability to communicate even with her own child had compounded her tragic failure as a mother."

Coast, whose newly founded, fast-growing cities were becoming beacons for restless Americans and immigrants alike. She spent some time in Seattle and then settled in San Francisco, supporting herself by giving piano lessons.

Professor W. H. Chaney, as he called himself, was born in Maine in 1821. By his mid-teens he had become a drifter, working at a variety of jobs. During the 1840s he was a schoolteacher and, according to his own account, a lawyer in West Virginia. About 20 years later he made the acquaintance of Luke Broughton, a professional astrologer —someone who claimed to be able to predict the future and tell people's fortunes by the positions of the planets. Chaney dedicated himself to astrology, which became his profession for the rest of his life. In 1869 he traveled to the West, leaving several former wives in the East. He lived for a time in Oregon, where, he later claimed, "U.S. Senators, Congressmen, Governors, Judges of the supreme and lower courts" were among the clients who sought his fortune-telling services. In 1873 he moved south to San Francisco, where he met Wellman.

In June 1874 Flora Wellman and W. H. Chaney began living together as a couple, although it is not clear whether they were ever married. Chaney lectured on science and astrology and told fortunes. He did not make much money at it, and he had plenty of competition. As the *Chronicle* dryly noted at the time, "Astrological knowledge is, of course, highly valuable, but the supply in San Francisco seems to be slightly in excess of the demand." Wellman continued to give piano lessons and also developed an occult sideline of her own. She ran sessions called séances, in which she claimed to communicate with spirits of the dead. This practice, known as spiritualism, was popular in the late 19th century; people attended séances in the hope of contacting loved ones who had died.

Chaney claimed to read the future, but he apparently failed to foresee one likely result of his relationship with

Joining the spiritualism craze of the late 19th century, Flora London claimed to be a medium who could communicate with the dead. The author of this pamphlet, "A. Medium," reveals the tricks used by some spiritualists to dupe their customers. Jack London held spiritualism in similar disdain.

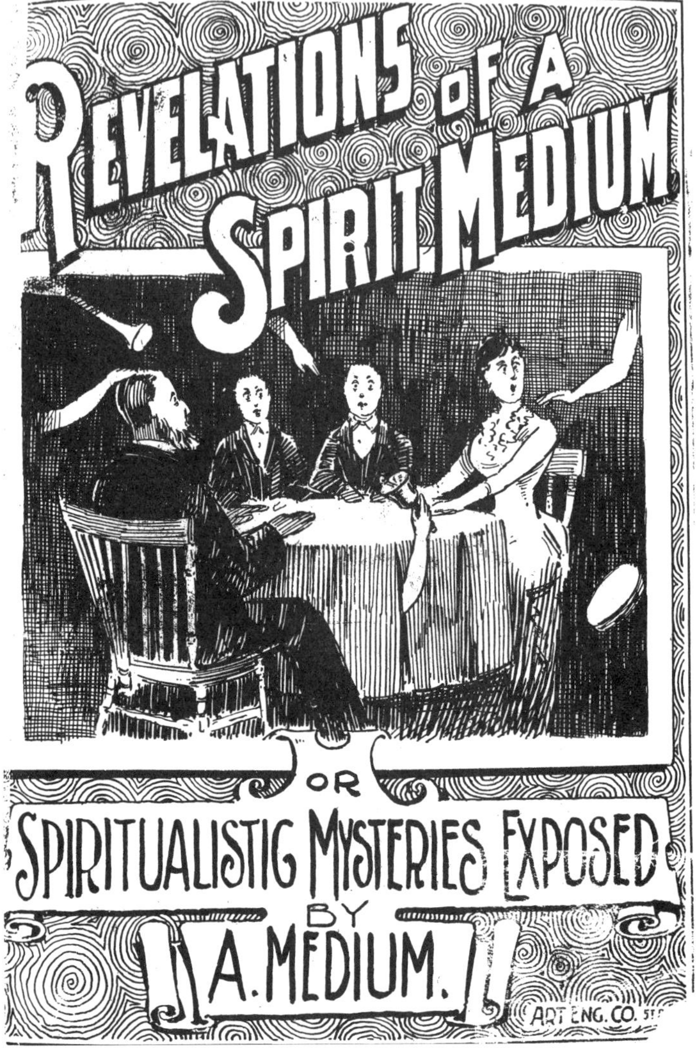

Wellman. She became pregnant. Chaney refused to believe that the child she was carrying was his, and he insisted that he would leave her unless she had an abortion. The result was a domestic upheaval that made the newspapers. On June 4, 1875, a story in the *Chronicle* was headlined "A Discarded Wife." According to the article, Chaney had driven Wellman out of their rented residence "for Refusing to Destroy Her Unborn Infant." Wellman then had tried to kill herself, first with a sleeping medicine and then with a pistol.

This scandalous affair did Chaney's reputation no good, and his astrological business failed completely. A short time later, before Wellman's child was born, he fled San Francisco and disappeared from Wellman's life. But she soon became acquainted with another man, and on September 7, 1876, when her baby John was eight months old, she married him. His name was John London. From that time forward Flora London's son would be known as Johnny or Jack London. He grew up thinking that John London was his biological father.

John London had been born in 1828 in rural Pennsylvania. When he was 20 he married and started a family. Like thousands of American families in the mid-19th century, the Londons migrated west in a series of moves, farming first in Illinois and then in Missouri. London served in the Union Army during the Civil War before settling with his family in Iowa. His wife died, and he was left with nine children to raise. It is unknown what became of most of these children, but they probably wound up living with relatives or neighbors, or in orphanages. London brought three of the children to California, seeking a climate that would benefit his son Charles, who had suffered a chest injury. But soon after the Londons reached the coast, the boy died.

When John London married Wellman his two daughters, Eliza and Ida, acquired a stepmother. Jack gained a stepfather and two older stepsisters. He was lucky in his new family. John London was a kind and affectionate parent who always treated Jack well, and Eliza became something of a mother to the little boy, reading to him and tending his childhood injuries with homemade remedies and gentle words. He would remain close to her all his life.

Even before Eliza came into his life, Jack had found a substitute mother in Virginia "Jennie" Prentiss, an African-American woman who nursed him after his birth. He spent most of his first year in the home of Prentiss and her husband Alonzo, who welcomed him lovingly. Later he would often spend stretches of time with the Prentisses, who called him Jackie—perhaps the source of the nickname by which everyone would one day know him.

It was fortunate for young Jack London that he had a kind stepfather, a motherly stepsister, and warm acceptance in the Prentiss family, because his relationship with his mother was distant and unloving. Flora London was temperamental, impulsive, and given to spending the family's limited funds on lottery tickets and get-rich-quick schemes that always failed. She also used claims of illness, including faked "heart attacks," to manipulate her family into doing what she wanted. John London was a man of quiet temper and poor health, having lost the use of one lung in the Civil War. For the sake of peace he generally gave his wife her way.

John London, Jack's stepfather, wears the star-shaped badge of a deputy constable, one of his occupations. Watching his worn-out stepfather scramble for work made Jack London fiercely determined not to become another "work-beast."

Jack's early childhood was shaped by the London family's scrambling efforts to find a place in the world and to make ends meet. When Wellman met John London, he was working as a carpenter, but the strain on his health forced him to seek a less physically demanding profession. He found work selling sewing machines door-to-door. Jack's mother still gave piano lessons when she could and also held séances in the London home. She claimed that a Native American spirit named Plume put her in touch with the dead, although her family disliked these spiritualist antics and Jack was frequently be embarrassed by them when he was growing up. Together John and Flora London earned enough money to maintain the family's shaky grasp on one of the lower rungs of the social ladder—but not enough to move up the ladder, as Flora was determined to do.

The Londons moved from one rented house or apartment to another every few months. In 1879 they crossed the bay from San Francisco to Oakland, where they again lived a nomadic life in a series of rented places. John London got hold of a few acres and began growing vegetables to sell, first to the local market and then in his own store. Although Flora's attempt to expand this business backfired and John lost the store, he had proved that he could make a living by farming. In 1881 he went to work on a larger piece of land outside the nearby city of Alameda. There he raised fruit and vegetables, and five-year-old Jack London started school.

At age nine, Jack London was photographed with his dog, Rollo. According to London's biographer Russ Kingman, Jack wanted the picture taken as a gift for his beloved stepsister Eliza.

CHAPTER

2

THE YOUNG PIRATE

Farming held little charm for young Jack, who later wrote that as a child he thought it was "the dullest possible existence." Flora London, however, was certain that her husband's green thumb would make their fortunes. She convinced him to move from Alameda and lease a 75-acre ranch south of San Francisco. Jack later described how the family moved to the ranch on his birthday in 1883: "We had horses and a farm wagon, and onto that we piled all our household belongings, all hands climbing up on the top of the load, and with the cow tied behind we moved 'bag and baggage' to the coast in San Mateo County, six miles beyond Colma."

John London planted potatoes and sold them in the small rural community of Colma. Jack rode along in the wagon as his father or another worker delivered the potatoes to town. Such trips usually involved a stop at a saloon, and these places seemed to the boy to be magical oases of good cheer. Jack would sit gratefully by the warmth of the stove and nibble a soda cracker while the men drank and laughed. On one memorable occasion a bartender gave Jack a sweet soft drink, and he was powerfully impressed by the kind gesture. Saloons, glowingly remembered as places of fellowship where cares could be forgotten, always had a strong attraction for Jack London.

Jack began his long battle with alcohol at an early age. Even as a very young child, he became violently drunk on two occasions. Once he drank the beer he was carrying to his father in the fields at the Alameda farm, and another time he drank great quantities of red wine at a wedding feast on a neighbor's ranch in San Mateo. Years later he wrote about how sick those episodes made him—yet they did not keep him from resuming his experiments in drinking in his middle teens.

If saloons and drunkenness hinted to the young Jack London of one path of escape from the hard work and boredom of everyday life, he soon discovered another road. The school he attended in San Mateo was rough; the teacher was a drunkard who was regularly beaten by his older students, after which he would vengefully beat the younger ones. Not surprisingly, this school offered little in the way of learning or inspiration. But less than a year after the Londons had moved to the leased ranch in San Mateo, John London had earned enough to make a payment toward a larger ranch of his own in the Livermore Valley southeast of Oakland, and the family moved back across the great bay. John London planted olive and fruit trees and built chicken coops, and Jack began attending a much better school. He had always liked to read, but now he discovered the wide horizons contained within the covers of books.

Jack's teacher loaned him Washington Irving's *Tales of the Alhambra,* the 19th-century American author's romantic stories about medieval Spain. He was so enraptured by these tales that he used old bricks to build a model of the Spanish castle-fortress called the Alhambra. Although the teacher never loaned him another book, as he secretly hoped she would, Jack read everything else he could find. His favorite book was *Signa,* by Marie Louise de la Ramée, a 19th-century English novelist who wrote sentimental and wildly popular tales under the pen name Ouida. Jack read and reread this story about an Italian peasant boy who rose above his crude origins, followed his dreams, and became a world-famous musician. Years later, at the peak of his own fame, Jack wrote that *Signa* had widened his vision of the world and "opened up to me the possibilities of the world of art. In fact it became my star to which I hitched my child's wagon." Remarkably, his copy of the book was missing the final 40 pages, and not until 1912—a year after he wrote the lines about the novel's importance to him—did he finally locate another copy of *Signa* and find out how the novel ended.

Life seemed to be going well for the Londons in Livermore, but Jack's mother wanted more money. Many people at the time shared their homes with boarders who paid for their rooms and meals, so she took Captain James Shepard, a 40-year-old Civil War veteran, and his two young daughters into the house. It was the teenaged Eliza, not Mrs. London, who did the extra work created by the boarders, but soon Eliza and Shepard fell in love, despite the difference in their ages. They married and moved to Oakland, depriving Mrs. London of both the income from the Shepards and Eliza's household services. The loss was even more crushing to eight-year-old Jack, who dearly loved his stepsister.

Another loss soon followed. At his wife's urging, John London had invested heavily in chickens, but a bird disease killed them all. With no money to pay the mortgage, the Londons lost their farm. Beaten and discouraged, John London wearily moved his family back to Oakland in 1885. To Jack's delight, they settled in a small cottage just two blocks from where the Shepards lived, and he could see all he wanted of Eliza.

In Oakland the Londons occupied a series of rented houses and moved often—four times in 1887 alone. Flora's piano lessons and séances continued, but John London, aging and in poor health and spirits, could find only part-time jobs as a night watchman or a deputy constable. To Flora's shame the family eventually wound up in West Oakland, one of the poorest parts of the city. She still gambled on the lottery and dreamed of winning a fortune, but in real life there was never enough money. Jack's stepsister Ida went to work as a laundress, and even as a child Jack was under constant pressure to work and contribute to the family's income. He carried newspapers, swept saloons, and helped the men who delivered ice to businesses and homes that had iceboxes (early refrigerators that used blocks of ice to keep things cool). Jack had been a shy boy, but on the rough-and-tumble streets of Oakland he developed into a sturdy, scrappy kid who could handle himself in a fight.

As a young man, Jack London looked back on his childhood and described its grimness in a letter to a friend: "Duty—at 10 years old I was on the streets selling newspapers. Every cent was turned over to my people, and I went to school in constant shame of the hats, shoes, clothes I wore. Duty—from then on I had no childhood. Up at three o'clock in the morning to carry papers. When that was finished I did not go home but continued on to school. School out, my evening papers. Saturday I worked on an ice wagon. Sunday I went to a bowling alley and set up pins for drunken Dutchmen. Duty—I turned over every cent and went dressed like a scarecrow."

During these years Jack's education continued in Oakland's primary schools. In West Oakland he attended Cole Grammar School. So did Priscilla Prentiss, the daughter of Jennie and Alonzo, who were now living in Oakland as well. Jack visited them often just as he continued to visit Eliza. He also made a lifelong friend at Cole—Frank Atherton, who later wrote a memoir titled *Jack London: Boyhood Adventures.* One of the happiest and most carefree times in Jack's childhood occurred in the summer of 1889, when the Athertons invited him to spend a few weeks with them in the country, near Auburn, California. Jack reveled

The Oakland Public Library opened the world of books to Jack London in the 1880s. London later wrote in John Barleycorn, *"I read mornings, afternoons, and nights. I read in bed, read at table, I read as I walked to and from school, and I read in recess while the other boys were playing."*

in the swimming, hiking, and especially the freedom from work and family responsibility.

Another source of joy was the Oakland Public Library. In this big, echoing building were all the books Jack could ever hope to read. Once he realized that he could actually take them home with him for free, he haunted the library and devoured volume after volume. His particular favorites were books about history and tales of exploration and adventure. He read during every single minute he could spare; once he beat up a school bully who teased him for reading during recess. Frank Atherton recalled that on one memorable occasion an explosion at a factory near Cole Grammar School caused all the teachers and students to run outside in a panic. Jack ran out, too—but he carried his library book with him.

Jack was fortunate to attract the attention of a librarian named Ina Coolbrith, who became his guide through the shelves of the Oakland Public Library. She was a friend of such famous authors as Mark Twain and Francis "Bret" Harte (who gained fame writing about the California mining camps), and she had helped to found a literary magazine

text continues on page 26

"DEADENING TOIL"

Jack London's 1913 book John Barleycorn *was primarily a meditation on the problems that alcohol—often referred to at the time as "John Barleycorn"—can cause. But, because much of what London had to say on the subject grew out of his own experiences, the book is also partly autobiographical. In this passage, he describes how stifled he felt while working in a pickle cannery as a teenager.*

I was barely turned fifteen, and working long hours in a cannery. Month in and month out, the shortest day I ever worked was ten hours. When to ten hours of actual work at a machine is added the noon hour; the walking to work and walking home from work; the getting up in the morning, dressing, and eating; the eating at night, undressing, and going to bed, there remains no more than the nine hours out of the twenty-four required by a healthy youngster for sleep. Out of those nine hours, after I was in bed and ere my eyes drowsed shut, I managed to steal a little time for reading.

But many a night I did not knock off until midnight. On occasion I worked eighteen and twenty hours on a stretch. Once I worked at my machine for thirty-six consecutive hours. And there were weeks on end when I never knocked off work earlier than eleven o'clock, got home and in bed at half after midnight, and was called a half-past five to dress, eat, walk to work, and be at my machine at seven o'clock whistle blow.

No moments here to be stolen for my beloved books. And what had John Barleycorn to do with such strenuous, Stoic toil of a lad just turned fifteen? He had everything to do with it. Let me show you. I asked myself if this were the meaning of life—to be a work-beast? I knew of no horse in the city of Oakland that worked the hours I worked. If this were living, I was entirely unenamoured of it. I remembered my skiff, lying idle and accumulating barnacles at the boat-wharf; I remembered the wind that blew every day on the bay, the sunrises and sunsets I never saw; the bite of the salt air in my nostrils, the bite of salt water on my flesh when I plunged overside; I remembered all the beauty and the wonder and the sense-delights of the world denied me. There was only one way to escape my deadening toil. I must get out and away on the water. And the way of the water led inevitably to John Barleycorn. I did not know this. And when I did learn it, I was courageous enough not to retreat back to my bestial life at the machine.

In the opening chapter of John Barleycorn, *London explains why he voted for woman suffrage despite his initial opposition to the amendment. He realizes that the accessibility of alcohol had given him the taste for it, and women, he reasons, will vote for prohibition and save coming generations from ever developing a taste for alcohol.*

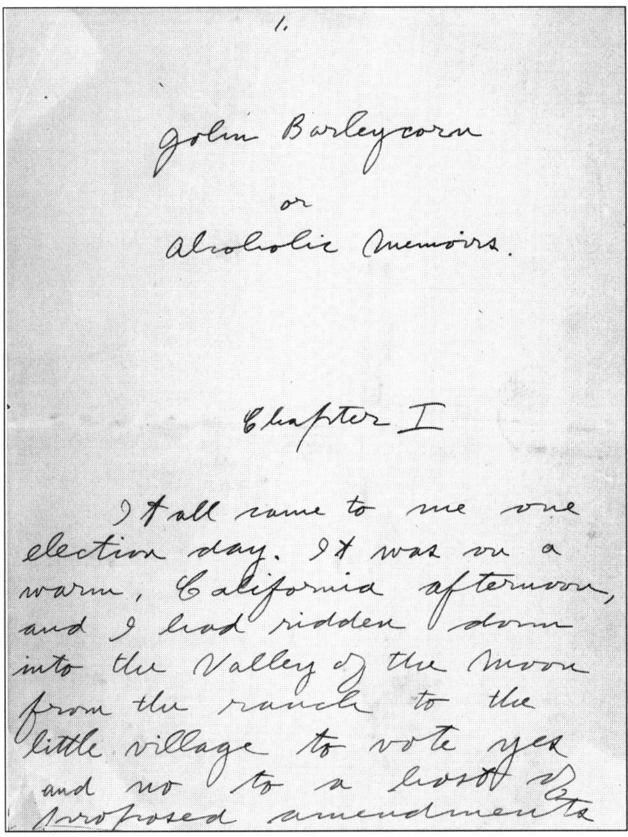

1.

John Barleycorn

or

Alcoholic Memoirs.

Chapter I

It all came to me one election day. It was on a warm, California afternoon, and I had ridden down into the Valley of the Moon from the ranch to the little village to vote yes and no to a host of proposed amendments called the *Overland Monthly,* of which Harte was the editor from 1868 to 1870. Later Coolbrith was named California's first poet laureate. Jack read the books she recommended, and he never forgot the kindhearted interest she had shown in him. The library would be an important part of Jack's life for many years. He later wrote in a letter to an admirer, "It was this world of books, now accessible, that practically gave me the basis of my education. Not until I began fighting for a living and making my first successes so that I was able to buy books for myself did I ever discontinue drawing many books on many library cards from out of the Oakland free public library."

Jack graduated from Cole in 1891. Instead of attending high school, he began working full time to help support his family. The best job he could find was at Hickmott's cannery, where he spent between 10 and 20 hours a day on his feet, stuffing pickles into jars as fast as his fingers could move. He earned 10 cents an hour. The work was physically exhausting and mentally numbing. In a story called "The Apostate," Jack later described a young man named Johnny who became a "work-beast" in a similar job: "There was no joyousness in life for him. The procession of the days he never saw. The nights he slept away in twitching unconsciousness."

One dream kept young Jack going. He had spent some happy hours with his father sailing a small boat called a skiff around San Francisco Bay. Now he ached to own such a boat—something that would give him a few precious hours of freedom in the clean, open world of sky and sea. He learned of a skiff he could buy for eight dollars. Through months of extra work and scrimping he managed to save five. Then one day Flora London showed up at the cannery and demanded that he give her the money. "I could have killed myself that night," he wrote a few years later in a letter to a friend. "After a year of hell... to be robbed of that petty joy."

By this time Jack London, at age 15, was becoming familiar with the seedy, exciting life of the waterfronts in Oakland and San Francisco. He would occasionally drink in the saloons, letting alcohol dull his cares and enjoying the talk of sailors, whalers, seal-hunters, and other seafarers. To the boy who felt imprisoned by factory toil these men's lives seemed grand and colorful. His favorite hangout was a place called Johnny Heinold's First and Last Chance Saloon in Oakland. Heinold remained Jack's friend for many years.

The bay was the setting for all kinds of maritime activities. Ships from around the world docked there, and smaller vessels busily crisscrossed its waters on local business: fishing, hauling goods between the towns around the bay, and pleasure cruising. One maritime activity that particularly fascinated Jack was oyster pirating. Bay oysters had become a valuable commodity. Operating by night, local men stole oysters from the oyster beds in the tidelands near San Mateo that were owned by the railroad companies and leased by big commercial fisheries. The pirates could make good money selling the stolen oysters to the local markets. Although oyster piracy was a crime punishable by imprisonment, many people sympathetically regarded the pirates as daring adventurers and admired them for tweaking the nose of big business. Jack heard about a sloop—a type of small boat perfect for oyster piracy—that he could buy for 300 dollars. He did not have that kind of money, but he knew someone who did. He borrowed the sum from Jennie Prentiss. The willingness of Jack's former nanny to lend him what was in those days a small fortune testifies to her affection for him.

With his sloop, the *Razzle Dazzle,* Jack became a pirate. A few years later, he boasted to a friend that he had made more money in a week stealing oysters than he could have earned in a year at the cannery. In reality, however, his earnings were less than he had hoped—and quite a bit of what he *did* make he spent in waterfront saloons. After a few months, a fire aboard the *Razzle Dazzle* made the boat unusable. For a time Jack worked on another oyster pirate's boat. He had realized, however, that life as a pirate was less glamorous and more dangerous than he had expected. When he was offered an opportunity to join the California Fish Patrol, he accepted.

The Fish Patrol had been formed to combat the very things that Jack and his friends had been doing—oyster pirating and other illegal fishing. The officer who offered Jack the job believed that no one would know more about how the pirates operated than a pirate. Jack's only pay was a share of the fines paid by the fishermen he arrested, but at least the job kept him free of time clocks and factory machines and allowed him to sail on his beloved bay. And there was no risk of being arrested.

However, the Fish Patrol was not without other dangers. Jack faced confrontations with the pirates, his former comrades, who carried knives and were not afraid to fight. On one occasion, Jack and his partner pretended to join a group of oyster pirates, only to trap and arrest them. Luckily, that confrontation ended peacefully, with the pirates' surrender. Alcohol proved to be a greater danger than angry pirates. The seagoing patrolmen drank at least as heartily as

The Oakland Harbor of the 1890s drew Jack London like a magnet. All his life London loved the waterfront, with its promises of open-air adventure, camaraderie among seamen, and escape from the humdrum life of the land-bound world.

the pirates, and the teenaged Jack found no shortage of opportunities to get drunk. He was slowly ruining his health, but drinking came close to killing him in a more sudden fashion. One night, after a drinking bout with his companions, he fell overboard. Seized by one of the many swift currents of the bay, he was borne out toward the sea. At first he was too drunk to panic, and he even enjoyed the experience of floating in the cool water under the stars. After a while he began to think of simply letting himself float out to sea—perhaps it would be better to end his dreary life now than to wait for alcohol, toil, and poverty to grind him into a broken old wreck like the bums who littered the waterfront. But as he sobered up, his love of life reasserted itself, and he began to fight the tides, struggling to swim for shore. Hours passed, and his strength was nearly drained when in the nick of time he was scooped from the sea into the boat of a passing fisherman. Jack had been lucky—not for the last time.

At 16, Jack left the Fish Patrol. He was restless and bored, but did not have another job or a plan for his future. Although he still lived at home, he became a waterfront loafer and spent much of his time in saloons. Later, in an autobiographical book called *John Barleycorn,* he described the sordid alcoholic binges from this period in his life. Some researchers and critics who have studied London feel that in *John Barleycorn* and other reminiscences he painted an exaggerated picture of his youthful drinking; others believe that the accounts he offered are substantially accurate. Either way, he was developing a drinking problem.

Around this time Jack fell in with a group of "road-kids," as he called them: homeless youths who rode the rails, hopping free—illegal and dangerous—rides on trains. They also begged for money, and sometimes they robbed people; London would later describe them as a pack of wolves. He joined their expeditions and became pretty good at panhandling, but to earn full membership in the road-kids group he had to ride the rails from California across the Sierra Nevada range to Nevada and back. He managed the dangerous leap onto the moving train, only to learn later that another road-kid who had tried to jump the same train had lost both legs. Jack, however, made the trip safely in both directions. The skills he honed with the road-kids would come in handy a few years later, when London bummed and begged his way across the United States.

To an observer of Oakland's waterfront dives in the 1890s, Jack London might have appeared to be on his way to becoming one of the lost souls whom he later portrayed in many of his works—a piece of human wreckage eking out a miserable, pinched existence illuminated only by health-destroying drinking bouts. Later in life he was to recall that all his acquaintances from the waterfront ended up prematurely dead or in jail, and to marvel at his own good fortune in escaping those fates. But something in Jack yearned to move in a more richly colored world, to explore the wide horizons about which he had read so much. The 13-year-old character named John would express those yearnings 20 years later in London's book *The Valley of the Moon:*

> Don't you sometimes feel you'd die if you didn't know what's beyond them hills an' what's beyond the other hills behind them hills? An' the Golden Gate! There's the Pacific Ocean beyond, and China an' Japan, an' India, an'. . . an' all the coral islands. You can go anywhere out through the Golden Gate—to Australia, to Africa, to the seal islands, to the North Pole, to Cape Horn. Why, all them places are just waitin' for me to come an' see 'em. I've lived in Oakland all my life, but I'm not going to live in Oakland the rest of my life, not by a long shot. I'm goin' to get away. . . away. . . .

And a week after his 17th birthday, in January 1893, Jack London *did* get away. Like many young men of his time, he went to sea. One of his tavern acquaintances was a sealer on a vessel that was spending a few months in port before making another seal-hunting voyage into the North Pacific. Fired by the idea of seeing the world and getting paid for it, Jack agreed to join him. He signed on as a crewman aboard the *Sophia Sutherland.*

The voyage across the Pacific took almost two months. It was an adventurous time for Jack. He loved traveling on the open sea, and he was thrilled by the sight of the mountains of Hawaii looming on the horizon as the ship passed. His duties were demanding and all the sailors worked extremely hard, but Jack did not have any difficulty mastering the shipboard tasks. His experience as the sailor of a small boat on the bay had prepared him for many aspects of seamanship and navigation—the biggest challenge was learning the names of the many lines, or ropes, that governed the operation of the sails on a three-masted schooner.

But there was also the challenge of making a place for himself as a rookie sailor in a crew full of tough, seasoned, older salts. He did this in two ways. First, he never shirked his work, and he made a point of helping out whenever there was work to be done in the maze of lines high above the rolling, pitching deck. Second, he used his fists. According to a 1900 interview that London gave to the *Overland Monthly,* he had won the respect of his shipmates by the ferocity with which he attacked an older man who tried to bully him. The men of the *Sophia Sutherland* learned that although they probably could beat Jack London in a fight, he would fight so wildly that he was bound to inflict damage on any opponent. They found that it was easier to leave him alone than to pick on him, and they soon accepted him into their company.

Jack saw plenty of ocean on the voyage, but he did not see much of the world. The first landfall was in the Bonin Islands, south of Japan, where sealing vessels landed to take on water. London recalled later, "It was my first foreign land; I had won to the other side of the world, and I would see all I had read in the books come true. I was wild to get ashore." But once he was ashore, he spent his entire leave in drunken revels with sailors from the many vessels that happened to be in port at the same time.

Leaving the Bonin Islands, the *Sophia Sutherland* sailed north for the cold, rough waters of the Bering Sea to harpoon seals and collect their hides. Even in summer the Bering Sea was a harsh environment. The men left the ship in small boats, working among ice flocs, tossed by giant waves. The slaughter that took place was harsher still. The ship was "covered with hides and bodies, slippery with fat and blood," as London would later write in his novel *The Sea-Wolf.* And on the blood-splattered deck the men worked "like butchers plying their trade, naked and red of arm and hand, hard at work with ripping and flensing knives, removing the skins from the pretty creatures they had killed."

After three months of this profitable butchery, the *Sophia Sutherland*'s hold was bulging with hides. The ship turned south to Yokohama, Japan, where the captain would sell the hides. Jack London saw no more of Japan, however, than he had seen of the Bonin Islands. The ship was in port for two weeks, which Jack spent in the waterfront saloons that catered to sailors. According to his account in *John Barleycorn,* the fun ended when the port police came after him. Fearing arrest for drunken, rowdy behavior, he dove into the water and swam a mile back to the ship.

From Yokohama the *Sophia Sutherland* headed back to San Francisco. There Jack engaged in one last drinking bout with his shipmates, but he managed to reach Oakland with some of his pay unspent. He bought a few cheap clothes for himself, and the rest of the money went to pay the family's most pressing bills. Jack London had spent nearly eight months at sea, and nothing had changed. He was still broke and drinking too much, and he still could not see a clear path to his future. But he now knew that he did not want to be a sealer—that was no road to a more noble existence, and his mother reminded him that the family needed his financial help more often than once a year.

Jack found a job in a factory that produced twine and coarse cloth from the fibers of the jute plant. The days were long and the work mindless. The pay was 10 cents an hour, the same amount he had earned in the cannery several years earlier. In the mid-1890s, a time of corporate greed, high unemployment, and worker unrest, there was a surplus of laborers with little formal education and only youth and physical strength to offer. Even Jack's modest hopes of advancement at the jute mill came to nothing. When his employers failed to give him a pay raise they had promised, he quit.

By that time, Jack had had his first taste of something more intoxicating than any liquor: success as a writer. His mother had noticed an announcement in the *Morning Call* of a contest for articles by writers under 22 years old, and she urged him to enter a description of one of the most exciting events of his sealing cruise. Jack spent three nights at the kitchen table, writing a rough draft and then polishing it, and Flora carried his article to the newspaper's offices.

On November 12, 1893, the *Morning Call* printed the winning essay: "Story of a Typhoon off the Coast of Japan," by 17-year-old John London, who had beaten out students at two of California's most prestigious universities, Stanford and the University of California at Berkeley. The prize was 25 dollars. This taste of success was so heady that Jack immediately sat down and hacked out a handful of other articles, all of which failed to sell. But although Jack could not yet earn a living as a professional writer, he had produced an essay that showed real talent. Crude as it is in some ways, "Typhoon" displays its author's gift for selecting colorful details that describe dramatic natural scenes, together with his interest in strong, simple emotions. These qualities would characterize all of Jack London's greatest works.

"Coxey's Army of the Unemployed" advances on Washington, D.C. Always eager for a change of scene, London joined a band of marchers from California but soon struck off on his own to see the country as a tramp, an experience he later described in The Road.

CHAPTER

3

The Road

After his experience at the jute mill, Jack London was determined not to settle for a life as an unskilled laborer. The new electrical power plants, he thought, were the way of the future. Unable to afford technical school, he decided to learn the electrical trade on the job. "I believed in the old myths which were the heritage of the American boy when I was a boy," he later wrote in *John Barleycorn*. "A canal boy could become president. Any boy who took employment with any firm, could, by thrift, energy, and sobriety, learn the business and rise from position to position until he was taken in as a junior partner. After that the senior partnership was only a matter of time." Bitter experience would soon show London just how hollow those myths were.

He took a job shoveling coal at a railway power plant. Not only did he learn nothing about the electrical trade, he exhausted himself with long hours of backbreaking toil until he learned from a coworker that the work he was doing had formerly been done by two men. London's strong young muscles were saving the railway company 50 dollars a month. He quit.

London was dismayed and disgusted by a world in which the owners of industries grew wealthy while workers slaved away in conditions that broke their spirits and bodies. He had seen John London searching desperately and often unsuccessfully for work, any work, that an aging man could do to bring in a few dollars. He himself was young and strong, and he had barely been getting by. What would happen when he could no longer be a "work-beast"? The U.S. government was many years from launching the social welfare programs that would eventually provide some help to the poor and those who could not work. In London's day it was every man for himself, with never enough jobs or money for those at the bottom of the heap.

London was not the only American distressed about this state of affairs. Jacob Coxey, a political activist, wanted to call public and government attention to the plight of the millions who were out of work. He organized "Coxey's Army of the Unemployed," a mass march from Ohio to Washington, D.C. Groups from around the country—including one from Oakland, led by a printer and labor organizer named Charles Kelly—planned to join Coxey's "army" in Washington. This, Coxey and others hoped, would stimulate Congress to pass bills authorizing highway and dam construction, which would provide jobs.

Jack London decided to join Kelly's "army," which was scheduled to leave Oakland in April 1894. At the time he was more interested in the potential for adventure than in labor organization or social issues, but he had nothing better to do. The previous year, he had traveled west across the ocean to see the world. Now he would head east to see his country. Later he wrote in *The Road*:

> Every once in a while, in newspapers, magazines, and biographical dictionaries, I run upon sketches of my life wherein, delicately phrased, I learn that it was in order to study sociology that I became a tramp. That is very nice and thoughtful of the biographers, but it is inaccurate. I

> became a tramp because—well, because of the life that was in me, of the wanderlust that was in my blood that would not let me rest...I went on "The Road" because I couldn't keep away from it; because I hadn't the price of a railroad fare in my jeans; because I was so made that I couldn't work all my life on "one same shift"; because —well, just because it was easier to than not to.

London missed the marchers' departure. He bought a train ticket to Sacramento, their first stop, with money that his stepsister Eliza had given him. He missed Kelly's group there, too—in fact, he did not catch up with them until Nevada. Drawing on his road-kid experience, London rode the rails most of the way. He kept a journal of some of his experiences that would come in handy later on, when he wrote *The Road*. In that book he gave an account of his experiences during this and later journeys. His travels that he began in pursuit of Kelly's "army" lasted eight months and took some unexpected—and unwelcome—turns.

Coxey's demonstration fizzled into a big bust. Hunger, exhaustion, lack of money, and the difficulties of travel caused so many men to desert from the "armies" that only 400 showed up in Washington. And even they drifted away after Coxey was arrested on the grounds of the Capitol. Long before then, however, Jack London had dropped out of Kelly's band. "I can't stand starvation," he wrote in his journal, and he headed to Chicago, traveling as a tramp, not a political protester. In Chicago, as in other cities he visited later on this trip, he got a good, close look at the dark underbelly of the United States while he passed through squatter camps inhabited by hoboes and the homeless. But he found one oasis of comfort in St. Joseph, Michigan, where he stayed for a few weeks with the family of Mary Everhard, his mother's sister, and became acquainted with a cousin named Ernest Everhard.

Leaving the Everhards, Jack jumped a boxcar and rode to Niagara Falls. He spent the evening watching the great falls, and then camped for the night in a nearby field. He rose early on June 29, planning to view the falls at sunrise. Instead he was arrested for vagrancy and hustled along to the city jail, where, to his amazement and horror, he was one of 16 hoboes who were swiftly sentenced to 30 days in the Erie County Penitentiary in Buffalo—without even the pretense of a trial. London was given no opportunity even to speak, much less to ask for the services of a lawyer. That injustice burned within him for years and helped fuel his belief that the country's political, economic, and social systems needed overhauling. In the meantime, however, he had to endure a month in what he called "a living hell."

London said later, when he wrote about that month in *The Road,* that most of his prison experience was too "unbelievable... unprintable... unthinkable" to commit to paper. Certainly he witnessed appalling sights of cruelty and degradation. He did write about how he became one of the 13 privileged prisoners called "hall men," whose job was to control the 500 vagrants jailed in the penitentiary's "bums' hall"—generally by beating them with fists or broom handles. He also described the system of graft, or corruption and bribery, by which the hall men stole a percentage of the food intended for the other prisoners and bartered with it for treats such as meat or books.

When his 30 days were over, London left Buffalo as fast as he could. Despite the "terrible scare" that prison had given him, he was still a tramp—in order to leave town he had to beg for money and then jump a boxcar. But prison *had* terrified London, forcing him to take a hard look at what he might become. As he explained later in an essay entitled "What Life Means to Me," he had been thrown from a fairly ordinary working-class background down into "the cellar of society, down in the subterranean depths of misery about which it is neither nice nor proper to speak... the pit, the abyss, the human cesspool, the shambles and the charnel house of our civilization.... the part of the edifice of society that society chooses to ignore." Jack London did not want to spend any more time in that pit. But he had begun to wonder how such conditions could exist and what society should do about them.

London spent that summer and fall riding the rails and seeing the sights, through Pennsylvania to Washington, D.C., then north to Baltimore, New York City, and Montreal, Canada. Along the way he had several close brushes with the law. Fearful of repeating his prison experience, he managed to talk or run his way out of trouble each time. He also encountered kindness, such as a meal served to him by two women in their dining room in Harrisburg, Pennsylvania, and the friendly advice he received from other tramps.

The Road, *London's account of the months he spent tramping the roads and riding the rails, first appeared as a series of articles in* Cosmopolitan *magazine. When it was published in book form, posed photographs illustrated some of the scenes and events London described, including this dangerous moment aboard a moving train.*

From Montreal, London turned west and made his way across Canada, hoping to reach the Pacific coast before winter. For one stretch of 1,000 miles he rode in a coal car, meditating on all that he had seen, done, and learned since leaving Oakland in April. He had discovered that not all "bums" were degenerates or alcoholics. Many were simply people too old, weak, sick, or disabled to work. Some were well educated. In Baltimore he had listened, ashamed of his ignorance, while hoboes and other soapbox orators debated politics, economics, and other intellectual topics about which he knew nothing. Why did society not offer such people something better than the hard and uncertain life of

text continues on page 42

A Tale of Two Hoboes

London's 1907 book The Road *told of his life as a hobo, riding the rails and seeing the country. This passage describes a bleak journey across Nevada and on to a small town in Wyoming, where London encountered a hobo acquaintance known as the Swede.*

I hit the high places across those hundreds of miles of Nevada desert, riding the overlands at night, for speed, and in the day-time riding in box-cars and getting my sleep. It was early in the year, and it was cold in those upland pastures. Snow lay here and there on the level, all the mountains were shrouded in white, and at night the most miserable wind imaginable blew off from them. It was not a land in which to linger. And remember, gentle reader, the hobo goes through such a land, without shelter, without money, begging his way and sleeping at night without blankets. This last is something that can be realized only by experience. . . .

Now it is no snap to strike a strange town, broke, at midnight, in cold weather, and find a place to sleep. The Swede hadn't a penny. My total assets consisted of two dimes and a nickel. From some of the town boys we learned that beer was five cents, and that the saloons kept open all night. There was our meat. Two glasses of beer would cost ten cents, there would be a stove and chairs, and we could sleep it out till morning. We headed for the lights of a saloon, walking briskly, the snow crunching under our feet, a chill little wind blowing through us.

Alas, I had misunderstood the town boys. Beer was five cents in one saloon only in the whole burg, and we didn't strike that saloon. But the one we entered was all right. A blessed stove was roaring white-hot; there were cosey, cane-bottomed arm-chairs, and a none-too-pleasant-looking barkeeper who glared suspiciously at us as we came in. A man cannot spend continuous days and nights in his clothes, beating trains, fighting soot and cinders, and sleeping anywhere, and maintain a good "front." Our fronts were decidedly against us; but what did we care? I had the price in my jeans.

"Two beers," said I nonchalantly to the barkeeper, and while he drew them, the Swede and I leaned against the bar and yearned secretly for the arm-chairs by the stove.

The barkeeper set the two foaming glasses before us, and with pride I deposited the ten cents. Now I was dead game. As soon as I learned my error in the price I'd have dug up another ten cents. Never mind if it did leave me only a nickel to my name, a stranger in a strange land. I'd have paid it all right. But that barkeeper never gave me a chance. As soon as his eyes spotted the dime I had laid down, he seized the two glasses, one in each hand, and dumped the beer into the sink behind the bar. At the same time, glaring at us malevolently, he said: —

"You've got scabs on your nose. You've got scabs on your nose. You've got scabs on your nose. See!"

I hadn't either, and neither had the Swede. Our noses were all right. The direct bearing of his words was beyond our comprehension, but the indirect bearing was clear as print: he didn't like our looks, and beer was evidently ten cents a glass.

I dug down and laid another dime on the bar, remarking carelessly, "Oh, I thought this was a five-cent joint."

"Your money's no good here," he answered, shoving the two dimes across the bar to me.

Sadly I dropped them back into my pocket, sadly we yearned toward the blessed stove and the arm-chairs, and sadly we went out the door into the frosty night.

But as we went out the door, the barkeeper, still glaring, called after us, "You've got scabs on your nose, see!"

I have seen much of the world since then, journeyed among strange lands and peoples, opened many books, sat in many lecture-halls; but to this day, though I have pondered long and deep, I have been unable to divine the meaning in the cryptic utterance of that barkeeper in Evanston, Wyoming. Our noses were all right.

a tramp? His own work experience in Oakland had taught him that willingness to labor almost to the point of collapse brought no real reward. Even those who mastered a trade could be thrown out of work in an instant by forces beyond their control. It seemed to him that life was a trap.

Yet perhaps there was a way out. London had already experienced the joy of earning money by writing. And in the past few months he had charmed people into giving him handouts—and on one occasion charmed a policeman out of arresting him—by spinning stories. In *The Road,* a book about his experiences, he was to say, "I have often thought that to this training of my tramp days is due much of my success as a story-writer. In order to get the food whereby I lived, I was compelled to tell tales that rang true. At the back door, out of inexorable necessity, is developed the convincingness and sincerity laid down by all authorities on the art of the short-story."

At age 18, London decided that he wanted to be neither a "work-beast" nor a tramp. "So I was resolved to sell no more muscle," he later wrote in an essay titled "How I Became a Socialist," "and to become a vendor of brains." But to earn a living with his mind he needed a better education than he possessed. He would not only go back to Oakland—he would go back to school as well. "I had been reborn," he wrote, "but not yet renamed, and I was running around to find out what manner of thing I was. I ran back to California and opened the books."

London reached Oakland in the winter of 1894, working his way south from Vancouver on Canada's Pacific coast by shoveling coal in a steamship. He settled into the family home, which by this time was in East Oakland, took on part-time jobs to help with the family finances, and prepared to enroll in Oakland High School in January 1895.

His stepsister Eliza lived nearby and, thoughtful and generous as always, helped enormously with his preparations. She bought him a table to study on, a bicycle to ride to school and to his evening jobs, and some much-needed dental work. The 19-year-old London had never owned a toothbrush or visited a dentist, and he had already lost several of his upper front teeth. Eliza paid to have false teeth made to replace the ones that were missing, and Jack bought his first toothbrush, hoping to save the rest.

Despite his eagerness to learn, London felt profoundly out of place in high school. At 19, after his hair-raising adventures, he was mingling with 15-year-olds, many of whom found him strange and shabby. Although he was in some ways a misfit, London found rewards in high school. For one thing, the school newspaper published 10 of his stories and essays on subjects as wide-ranging as the Bonin Islands, tramping, and a murder mystery. One of these tales, called "One More Unfortunate," is about a man who, inspired by the novel *Signa,* London's own boyhood favorite, becomes a violinist. But he spends his time playing in saloons and cheap music halls, until one night, crushed by the realization that he has wasted his talent and his life, he drowns himself. London received no pay for these pieces, but they provided excellent opportunities to polish his skills. He signed the first story "John London" but then switched to "Jack London," the name he would use for the rest of his life.

London also participated enthusiastically in the activities of a local speech club, the Henry Clay Debating Society, many of whose members were university students. Through reading and discussion, as well as the actual speech-making, the club broadened London's knowledge and sharpened his communications skills. He also made a good friend, a fellow debater named Ted Applegarth. London became friendly with Ted's family, who had recently moved from England to California, and he eagerly absorbed the cultured, artistic atmosphere of the Applegarth home. He also developed an intense crush on Ted's sister Mabel, a university student who was several years older than Jack. London spent part of the summer of 1895 vacationing with the Applegarths in the Yosemite Valley of the Sierras before resuming high school and work in the fall.

London explored other sources of intellectual stimulation and expression during this time. The Oakland Public Library remained a beloved haunt—in fact, it was his old friend, librarian Ina Coolbrith, who had introduced him to Fred Jacobs, a scholarly young man who invited London to join the debating society. Another librarian, Frederick Irons Bamford, also took an interest in London, frequently recommending books and then discussing them with him over lunch. London devoured the major scientific, political, and economic works of the time: Charles Darwin's *On the Origin of Species,* which introduced the new biological concept of the evolution of species; Karl Marx and Friedrich Engels's *The Communist Manifesto,* which interpreted history as the war between socioeconomic classes and presented a vision of society shaped by socialist principles of equality; and Herbert Spencer's *First Principles,* which mingled biology, science, history, and sociology in a philosophy that offered the prospect of human progress and even perfection. At the time these were new, revolutionary, ideas, and they were reshaping the thinking of people around the world. London thrived on the sense that his mind was expanding, that he was in touch with important things, and that he was finally becoming a person of brain, not brawn.

He allied himself with the socialist cause, joining the local branch of the Socialist Labor Party in 1896. He earned the nickname "boy socialist" as he tried to explain what he meant by socialism through speeches he made in City Hall Park and letters that he published in the newspapers. London was not drawn to socialism by grand, abstract theories or even a new vision of history. He believed—based on things he had seen and experienced—that society was unfair to those at the bottom, and he thought that socialism would spread opportunity more fairly and relieve the worst sufferings caused by poverty and ignorance. He once claimed that anyone was a socialist who worked toward a better system of government than the one under which he lived. Although London's relationship with the Socialist Labor Party changed over the years, he always firmly believed in equality of economic and social opportunity and in universal education.

In January 1896, a year after he started high school, London turned 20 and quit. He felt out of place and impatient, and he believed he could make faster progress studying on his own. His goal was college, and he knew that if he could pass an entrance exam he could be admitted to the University of California at Berkeley without completing high school. He embarked on a frenzy of studying, eventually reading for 19 hours a day, trying to cram his brain full of knowledge about English, physics, math, and history—the subjects that would be tested in Berkeley's entrance exams in August. "My body grew weary, my mind grew weary, but I stayed with it," London later wrote of this feverish time in *John Barleycorn*. "My eyes grew weary and began to twitch, but they did not break down." Mabel Applegarth, Fred Jacobs, and another friend named Bessie Maddern helped by tutoring him in various subjects. At last London rode his bicycle to Berkeley to begin the three days of testing, only to find the exams far more difficult than the samples he had seen. Later he learned that Berkeley had chosen that year to raise its test standards considerably.

When the ordeal of the tests was finished, so was London. He never wanted to see another book, much less read one. With some food and a blanket he wandered down to the waterfront, borrowed a small boat, and sailed out onto the bay. He wanted to get drunk—and soon he encountered old comrades from the Fish Patrol, who were happy to buy as many drinks as he could swallow. After that spree London cruised on the bay for a week, revisiting old haunts and basking in the beauty of water and sky, before going home to see how he had done in the exams.

The Applegarth family invited 19-year-old London (standing, top left) to join them on a vacation in Yosemite Valley. One of the few carefree times in the hard-working young man's life, the vacation gave him a lifelong love of wilderness recreation.

CHAPTER

The Northland

London's cramming had paid off. He had passed the exams, and in the fall of 1896 he entered the University of California at Berkeley, bicycling between the campus and his home in Oakland. College, London had decided, was going to teach him how to be a "brain merchant"—how to earn his living by writing. He started with several courses each in English and history.

Despite his high hopes, London was disappointed by college. He was so busy that he had little time to spend with Mabel Applegarth and his other friends, and he missed them. And although he made some new friends at Berkeley, for the most part he felt out of place among the young middle-class men and women of the student body, whose privileged lives, London was keenly aware, had been very different from his own rough existence. Most frustrating was the fact that he was not receiving the stimulation he had expected from his classes, his professors, and the university in general. The intellectual excitement he had found in the debating society and the socialist movement seemed lacking at Berkeley.

London felt the same eager impatience he had experienced after returning to high school—the certainty that a world of knowledge lay waiting for him and that he could explore it more quickly on his own than sitting in a classroom. On top of everything else, the London family's finances were as shaky as ever. Jack had probably borrowed money from his stepsister Eliza to pay the university's fees, but he could not continue to do so. At the same time, his mother needed his help with the household expenses. For all these reasons London withdrew from the university in February 1897, a few weeks into his second semester. He hoped to return one day to earn the diploma that commanded so much respect in society, but he never did.

The "boy socialist" remained as active in the Bay Area's socialist movement as ever—his arrest for public speechmaking in Oakland came less than a week after he left Berkeley. At the same time, however, London channeled much of his energy into a burst of writing, certain that he could earn more money as a published author than through physical labor. For several months he plunged into a frenzy of writing that was as all-consuming as his period of cramming for the Berkeley entrance exams had been the previous summer.

Later, in *John Barleycorn,* London described this no-holds-barred attempt to win a foothold in the world of publishing:

> Heavens, how I wrote! . . . The way I worked was enough to soften my brain and send me to a mad-house. . . . I wrote everything—ponderous essays, scientific and sociological, short stories, humorous verse, verse of all sorts. . . . On occasion I composed steadily, day after day, for 15 hours a day. At times I forgot to eat, or refused to tear myself away from my passionate outpouring in order to eat.

London had once dreamed of becoming a musician, perhaps because of the influence of his beloved *Signa,* the story of a musician. However, by age 20, he had come to believe that he possessed real talent as a writer, and he decided to focus on three kinds of writing: poetry first, followed by essays on philosophical or political topics, then "last, and least, fiction writing." He laboriously wrote all his compositions in longhand and then typed them on a borrowed typewriter that, he later recalled in *John Barleycorn,* "must have been a first model in the year one of the typewriter era." This balky machine seemed to be possessed by "an evil spirit." To operate it London had to pound its keys so hard that his fingers blistered and bled.

London sent manuscript after manuscript to magazines in the big East Coast cities where American literary activity was concentrated. Every one of them returned to Oakland, rejected by the publishers—"My manuscripts made amazing round-trip records between the Pacific and the Atlantic," he was to say. But poems, essays, and stories were not the only things London wrote during this period. He also wrote several letters to W. H. Chaney.

No one knows whether Jack London had earlier discovered that his mother and John London were not married at the time of his birth. Even if this were the case, he probably grew up thinking London was his father anyway. But when Jack London was 21 someone told the him that John London was not his father. Jack crossed the bay to San Francisco and pored through old newspaper files to learn the truth. There he found a notice of his birth to "the wife of W. H. Chaney" and also the shocking article about Chaney's demand for an abortion and Flora Wellman's subsequent suicide attempts. Chaney was sufficiently well known as an astrologer for London to locate his address in Chicago, where he had been living for some years. In May and June 1897 London wrote to Chaney, asking if Chaney was his father.

Chaney responded with two letters in which he denied being London's father. He admitted that he had lived with London's mother but claimed that they had never married and that he had been sexually impotent while they were together. "Therefore I cannot be your father, nor am I sure who your father is," wrote Chaney, who went on to suggest that London's mother had sexual relationships with several other men while he knew her. No evidence supports Chaney's accusations. Most researchers are convinced that Chaney was indeed Jack London's father and that London himself believed this to be true. It appears, however, that London never contacted Chaney again. He had kept their correspondence secret from his mother, to spare her feelings, and during the rest of his life he never mentioned Chaney and always spoke of John London as his father.

Forced to take a job to earn some money for the family, Jack London next put in several months of hard labor at a school laundry. When the school closed in June, he looked around for a job that would leave him a little time and energy for writing. Despite his failure to sell any of his work, London had not given up on his dream. "My career was retarded, that was all. Perhaps I did need further preparation. I had learned enough from the books to realize that I had touched on the hem of knowledge's garment," he wrote in *John Barleycorn,* years later. "My waking hours, and most of the hours I should have used for sleep, were spent with the books." At this point London had a burning desire to write and had begun to master the necessary skills. All he needed was the right subject, and he was about to discover it.

In July 1897, ships from Alaska docked in San Francisco and Seattle. They carried dozens of jubilant miners, several tons of gold, and the first word of a momentous discovery. Gold had been found along the Klondike River, a tributary of the Yukon River in northwest Canada. The Klondike gold rush, called "the last and most frenzied of the great international gold rushes" by Canadian historian Pierre Berton, had begun.

The telegraph wires and newspapers spread word of the gold strike, igniting fantasies of instant wealth. Almost literally overnight, thousands of men—and a few women—

from the United States and other countries were headed north to a wild and inhospitable land where they believed they would find fist-sized nuggets of gold lying on the ground for the taking. The transforming power of gold turned the Klondike, an almost uninhabited wilderness, into a household name around the world. It turned Dawson City on the Yukon River from a small, isolated outpost into a boomtown of 30,000 people, its mud streets lined with saloons, banks, brothels, stores, and miners' tents—"a wild, picturesque, lawless mining camp.... a picture of blood and glittering gold-dust, starvation, and death," as one U.S. marshal there recalled. The gold rush made a handful of prospectors into millionaires and the rest into ragged, hungry, discouraged wretches. And it would make Jack London into a successful writer.

Jack London was one of many people in the American West who came down with an instant and severe case of gold fever. So did his stepsister Eliza's husband, Captain James Shepard. The two set out for Alaska together, with the captain paying their traveling expenses. Like many who went north, London was very likely drawn by more than the lure of gold. Gold rushers also felt the attraction of the wilderness, of adventure, and of a place that seemed to be a true frontier, something that had vanished from the civilized United States by the end of the 19th century. Writer Hamlin Garland, who also joined the Klondike gold rush, described that allure in *The Trail of the Goldseekers* (1899): "I believed it to be the last march of the kind which could ever come to America, so rapidly were the wild spaces being settled up.... I wished to return to the wilderness also, to forget books and theories of art and social problems, and come again face to face with the great free spaces of woods, skies, and streams." In his writing, London would capture something of this wild, free, stern spirit.

London and Shepard got an early start. Less than two weeks after news of the gold strike arrived, they sailed north from San Francisco. They became friends with shipboard companions named Merrit Sloper, Fred Thompson, and Jim Goodman, with whom London would travel for many weeks and many miles. Thompson's diary sheds light on these months of London's life.

London's journey to the Klondike was appallingly—and typically—difficult. Although the Klondike lay in Canada, few of the gold rushers tried to reach it by an overland journey through the Canadian Rockies. Nearly all of them followed the route taken by London and Shepard, sailing to the southeastern coast of Alaska and then crossing one of the two passes that led through the Coast Mountains into the interior of that remote, rugged corner of North America.

The ship that carried London and his comrades north ended its run at Juneau, Alaska. There the miners hired Native Americans to carry them and their equipment in 70-foot canoes another 100 miles north to Dyea, a settlement at the base of the Chilkoot Pass, one of the two passes through the Coast Mountains. London wrote to Mabel Applegarth from Dyea:

> Had a pleasant time. The 100 miles lay between mountains which formed a Yosemite Valley the whole length, & in many places the heights were stupendous. Glaciers and waterfalls on every side. Yesterday a snow slide occurred & the rumble & roar extended for fully a minute.

From Dyea the prospectors had to make their way along a rough eight-mile trail to the horribly steep three-quarter-mile Chilkoot Pass. At the top of the pass were officials of the Canadian Mounted Police who made certain that everyone who crossed had enough food and supplies to live on for a year—normally about a ton of goods for each person. Travelers who wanted to go to the Klondike had to haul their gear up the pass in load after backbreaking load. Jack London calculated that for every mile of the pass he actually traveled between 20 and 30 miles, often carrying a pack that weighed 75 pounds.

Alaska's steep and brutally difficult Chilkoot Pass was the gateway to the Klondike gold fields. London joined the estimated 20,000 to 30,000 gold seekers who swarmed to the Klondike in the first year of the gold rush.

Even before getting to Chilkoot, the middle-aged Shepard realized that he could not complete the trip, and he had turned back. London and the others continued, clawing their way to the top of the pass again and again with heavy loads. By the end of August they had managed to get everything to the summit. From there they had to haul it another 15 miles to Lake Linderman, where they would have to build boats to float across the lake and north down the Yukon River into the Klondike region. The journey would be a dreary rain-soaked race against the bitter snows and brutal cold of winter, which sets in early in that part of the world. Exhausted and in despair, many gave up while climbing the pass or slogging along the trail. They wept and wailed, somberly turned to retrace their steps, or simply blew out their brains and fell at the trailside. London and his friends kept going. By the middle of September they had built two 27-foot boats and were ready to begin the next stage of their journey, a voyage of nearly 400 miles.

The upper Yukon River rages through several narrow canyons and has many hazardous rapids. Some travelers portaged (carried their boats and gear) around the rapids, but London's party had no time to spare, so they ran several of the river's worst rapids. London's experience as a small-boat sailor served them well. He not only guided their craft successfully through treacherous stretches of the river—including one place where they watched helplessly as two other boats overturned and their crews drowned—but he also steered the boat of a family that was following his group down the river through several canyons.

By the beginning of October they were racing against winter, and winter was winning. Every day the Yukon was a little slushier as the winter ice began to form. When London's group reached Upper Island at the mouth of the Stewart River, about 70 miles south of Dawson City, they decided to spend the winter there in some abandoned cabins. London staked a mining claim to a piece of land along nearby Henderson Creek, literally driving wooden stakes into the ground to mark the boundaries of the land he wanted to claim. This did not, however, give him ownership of the land. He could not consider it his until he had his claim registered with the Canadian authorities and paid a fee. The river remained open long enough for London and his companions to make a quick trip to Dawson to register their claims and get a look at the place that would soon be calling itself the "Paris of the North." In Dawson, London formed a friendship with two brothers named Bond, who came from a ranch near Santa Clara, California. He particularly admired their dog Jack, a mix of Saint Bernard and collie. A few years later that dog would be the model for Buck, the canine hero of London's greatest and best-known work of literature, *The Call of the Wild.*

Meanwhile, London returned to Upper Island for the winter, which he later described as "40 days in a refrigerator." Actually, the winter was far longer than that. London spent part of the time in a cabin on the island and part of it in a cabin on Henderson Creek, where the group had laid their gold claims. If London found any gold there, it was not much. The real treasure was in the observations he made and the stories he heard. He met and talked with American Indians, prospectors from all kinds of backgrounds, marshals and mounted police, and hunters. He learned about the harsh realities of life in the Northlands. For example, he heard about a man caught outdoors in the bitter cold whose fingers froze before he could make a lifesaving fire. London later told that story in "To Build a Fire," one of his most widely read tales. He formed a lasting admiration for men

A log found in London's cabin on Henderson Creek bears the words "Jack London, Miner, Author, Jan 27, 1898." London may have scrawled them during the winter of 1897–98, but it is possible that someone else wrote them later, when London was famous.

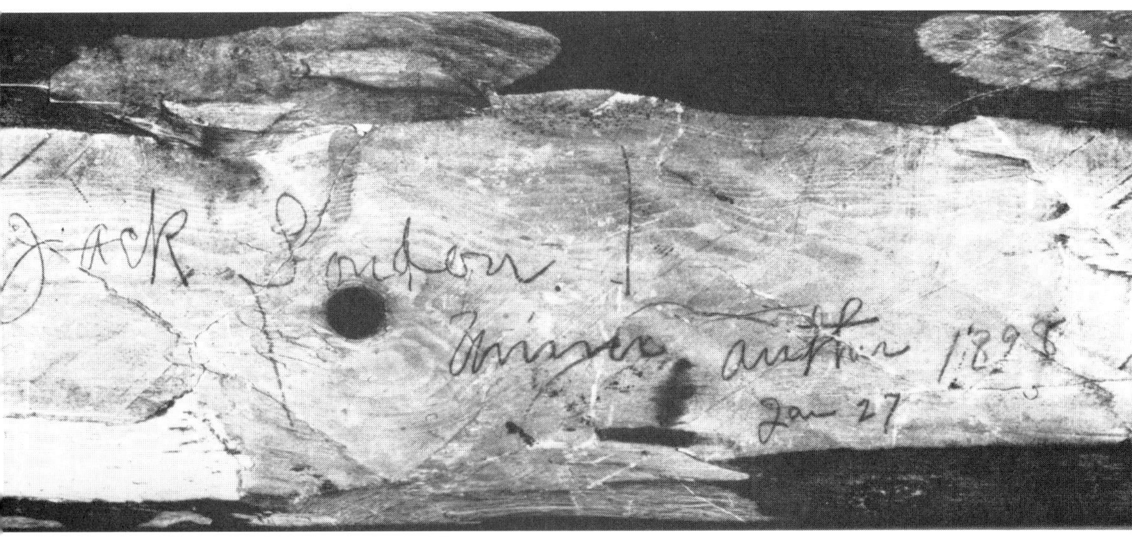

text continues on page 58

HOUSEKEEPING IN THE KLONDIKE

Jack London drew upon his brief time in the Yukon for years' worth of writing material. Much of what he wrote about the Northland was stern and serious, but he occasionally took a humorous tone when describing the life of the miners there. This passage comes from "Housekeeping in the Klondike," an article published in Harper's Bazaar *magazine in 1900.*

Housekeeping in the Klondike—that's bad! And by *men*—worse. Reverse the proposition, if you will, yet you will fail to mitigate, even by a hair's-breadth, the woe of it. It is bad, unutterably bad, for a man to keep house, and it is equally bad to keep house in the Klondike. That's the sum and substance of it. Of course men will be men, and especially this is true of the kind who wander off to the frozen rim of the world. The glitter of gold is in their eyes, they are borne along by uplifting ambition, and in their hearts is a great disdain for everything in the culinary department except "grub." "Just so long as it's grub," they say, coming in off trail, gaunt and ravenous, "grub, and piping hot."

... Yes, it would seem a pleasant task to cook for such men; but just let them lie around cabin to rest up for a week, and see with what celerity they grow high-stomached and make sarcastic comments about the way you fry the bacon or boil the coffee. And behold how each will spring his own strange and marvelous theory as to how sour-dough bread should be mixed and baked. Each has his own recipe (formulated, mark you, from personal experience only), and to him it is an idol of brass, like unto no other man's, and he'll fight for it—ay, down to the last wee pinch of soda—and if need be, die for it. If you should happen to catch him on trail, completely exhausted, you may blacken his character, his flag, and his ancestral tree with impunity; but breathe the slightest whisper against his sour-dough bread, and he will turn upon and rend you.

. . . The cold, the silence, and the darkness somehow seem to be considered the chief woes of the Klondiker. But this is all wrong. There is one woe which overshadows all others—the lack of sugar. Every party which goes north signifies a manly intention to do without sugar, and after it gets there bemoans itself upon its lack of foresight. Man can endure hardship and horror with equanimity, but take from him his sugar, and he raises his lamentations to the stars. And the worst of it is that it all falls back upon the long-suffering cook. . . . Such a cook must be a man of resources. Should his comrades cry out that vinegar be placed upon the beans, he must know how to make it out of water, dried apples, and brown paper. He obtains the last from the bacon-wrappings, and it is usually saturated with grease. But that does not matter. He will easily learn that in a land of low temperatures it is impossible for bacon grease to spoil anything. It is to the white man what blubber and seal oil are to the Eskimo. Soul-winning gravies may be made from it by the addition of water and browned flour over the fire. Some cooks base far-reaching fame solely upon their gravy, and their names come to be on the lips of men wherever they foregather at the feast.

and women strong enough to test themselves and to survive in the most grueling circumstances. And he was awed by the emptiness and loneliness of the great northern spaces, by what he called "the White Silence" in a short story by that name: "It is not pleasant to be alone with painful thoughts in the White Silence. The silence of gloom is merciful, shrouding one with protection and breathing 1,000 intangible sympathies; but the bright White Silence, clear and cold, under steely skies, is pitiless."

Rex Beach, a journalist who joined the gold rush and later became a popular writer of adventure novels, wrote dismissively of the Klondike in his autobiography: "There's no drama up here, no comedy, no warmth. Life is as pale and as cold as the snow... we'll never read any great stories about Alaska and the Klondike. This country is too drab and weary." Jack London, who would prove Beach spectacularly wrong, found in the Klondike the material of great stories and in himself the makings of a storyteller. "It was in the Klondike that I found myself," he said in a pamphlet titled *Jack London by Himself.* "There, nobody talks. Everybody thinks. You get your perspective. I got mine."

London also, unfortunately, got scurvy, a disease the miners called "Arctic leprosy." Caused by a severe shortage of vitamin C, scurvy has dire results: bleeding gums, loose teeth, sore joints, lameness, and eventually death. In June 1898, just as fresh hordes of hopeful prospectors were getting ready to storm the passes in Alaska, London built a raft and floated downstream to Dawson City. He received some vitamin-rich vegetables in a hospital there, but his money was almost gone. He knew that he must either get a job or head for home. London spent a few weeks absorbing the sights and characters of Dawson—saloons, fistfights, dancers and prostitutes, old-timers fallen on hard times, and newcomers filled with ignorance and optimism. Then he and two friends, John Thorson and Charley Taylor, pooled their funds, bought a small and leaky skiff, and set out on the

During his long voyage down the Yukon River, London caught many glimpses of Native Americans like these two. Within a few years, London would draw on his impressions of these people and their life in the vast and lonely Northland for the themes and settings of the stories collected in Children of the Frost *and* God of His Fathers.

Yukon for the 1,800-mile trip north to St. Michael, Alaska, a port on the Bering Sea at the Yukon's mouth.

Although he suffered increasingly from his scurvy, London kept a journal of that Yukon journey. He wrote of passing mysteriously abandoned Native American villages, of witnessing strange religious rites as they passed other settlements, of going almost mad from the constant attacks of huge swarms of bloodthirsty mosquitoes, and of white men met deep in the wilderness, at home with their American Indian wives. He also wrote of a kind missionary who gave him some potatoes and a can of tomatoes to help his scurvy. The vegetables were worth more to him by that time than the richest gold claim.

At the end of June the travelers reached St. Michael and took passage on a ship headed south. Before long London was home again in Oakland. He was broke, depressed, and still sick. He was also grieving, for he learned that John London had died the previous October, while Jack was struggling toward Dawson. London's friend Fred Jacobs also died in 1898. London remained friendly with Bessie Maddern, who had been engaged to Jacobs.

Flora London may have been disappointed to see her son return from the Klondike without a bulging bag of gold, but she expected him to get a job at once to help support her and young Johnny Miller, the son of her stepdaughter Ida. The boy now lived with Flora and was another responsibility for Jack, who applied for many jobs but had no success. He needed money, so he pawned his most treasured possessions: his bicycle, a raincoat that John London had left to him, and a watch that Captain Shepard had given him. Eventually he applied for a job at the post office.

During these months, and while he was waiting to hear from the post office, London once again launched himself into a flurry of writing. He offered an article about his Yukon journey to the *San Francisco Bulletin,* which rejected it because "interest in Alaska has subsided." As he had done the previous year, he bombarded magazine editors with scores of stories, poems, essays, and jokes. He studied books about writing and the works of authors he admired, trying to discover just what made good writing good. And once again he collected a big pile of rejection slips, the notes that publishers and editors send to authors when returning work they do not care to publish.

Ironically, one of London's stories had already been published—but he did not know it. In the fall of 1897, while London was laboring to reach the Yukon, *Owl Magazine* had printed a story of his called "Two Gold Bricks." Not only did he receive no payment for the story, he never even knew that it had been published. A year later, he was still a struggling, unpublished writer. Finally, in December 1898, he received word from the *Overland Monthly* that it would publish one of his stories, "To the Man on the Trail." To London's dismay, though, the magazine offered him only 5 dollars; he had been hoping for eight times that. In the weeks that followed he came very close to absolute despair. In a letter to Ted Applegarth, he confessed, "I have never been so hard up in my life."

Early in 1899, however, he received a more generous reward for his hard work. *The Black Cat,* a literary magazine, offered him 40 dollars for his story "A Thousand Deaths." London was forever grateful to the editor, whom he said had saved his career. Soon the *Overland Monthly* was offering to buy more stories, not for much money, but it was a start.

ON PIGEON RIVER. Prize Story.

The Black Cat

May 1899

On Pigeon River.
$250 Prize Story.
Jeanie Drake.

The Dutchman's Mine.
Harry B. Tedrow.

In the Service of the Czar.
Walter Laurence Hackett.

Miss Wilmarth's Little Luncheon.
Margaret Dodge.

A Thousand Deaths.
Jack London.

5 CENTS

No. 44. Copyright, 1899, by The Shortstory Publishing Co.

THE SHORTSTORY PUBLISHING CO 144 HIGH ST BOSTON.MASS.

The Black Cat *magazine published Jack London's story "A Thousand Deaths" in this issue. Years later, in the introduction to a collection of stories from the magazine, London told what the sale had meant to him: "I was at the end of my tether, beaten out, starved. . . . Literally, and literarily, I was saved by the* Black Cat *story."*

Just at this time London faced a very important decision. A job as a mail carrier became available at the post office. Should he take it or not? On one hand lay steady, if uninspiring, work. On the other lay the risky but intoxicating prospect of being a professional writer. London talked to the postmaster and explained his position. He suggested that perhaps someone else could take this job, giving London a little more time to succeed with his writing, and then London could have the next job that became available if he still was interested. But the postmaster stubbornly insisted that if London wanted to work for the post office he would take the job that he was offered, and that was that. London became angry and declared, "I won't take it." Right or wrong, he had made his choice. Now he had to hope that he would, as he put it in *John Barleycorn,* "win out at writing."

Soon London had evidence that he was on the right track. The *Atlantic Monthly,* the nation's leading literary magazine, accepted a story called "An Odyssey of the North" and paid him 120 dollars. London was on his way. By the end of the year he had signed a contract with a publishing company for his first book, a collection of stories that would be called *The Son of the Wolf.* Jack London's earnings as a writer during 1899 averaged almost 30 dollars a month, about what he had been earning in his last regular job, at the school laundry.

When the new century dawned in 1900, Jack London was earning his living, as he had long hoped to do, with his brain and his pen, not his muscles and sweat. His agonizing efforts to educate himself, the long hours of poring over philosophy and science and literature, the strict writing schedule he had kept and the game he made of learning as many new words as possible—all these were finally bearing fruit. But it was his ability to describe the landscapes, the people, and the harsh yet pure realities of life in the Klondike that first won London an audience.

One reader who was impressed with London's early work was Cloudesley Johns, a young man who also hoped to be a writer. He wrote to London, striking up a correspondence that blossomed into a lifelong friendship. Much of what we know about London's writing habits comes from the many letters he sent to Johns throughout his career. In one he tried to pass along to Johns what he had learned about writing: "Don't you tell the reader. Don't. Don't. Don't. But have your characters tell it by their deeds, actions, talk, etc.... And get the atmosphere. Get the breadth and thickness to your stories, not only the length." In another he described his schedule: "Am now doing a thousand words a day, six days a week.... I have made it a rule to make up next day what I fall behind; but when I run ahead, not to permit it to count on the following day. I am sure a man can turn out more, and much better in the long run working this way, than if he works by fits and starts." The next few years would prove just how much London could "turn out" now that he had finally cracked open the door to success.

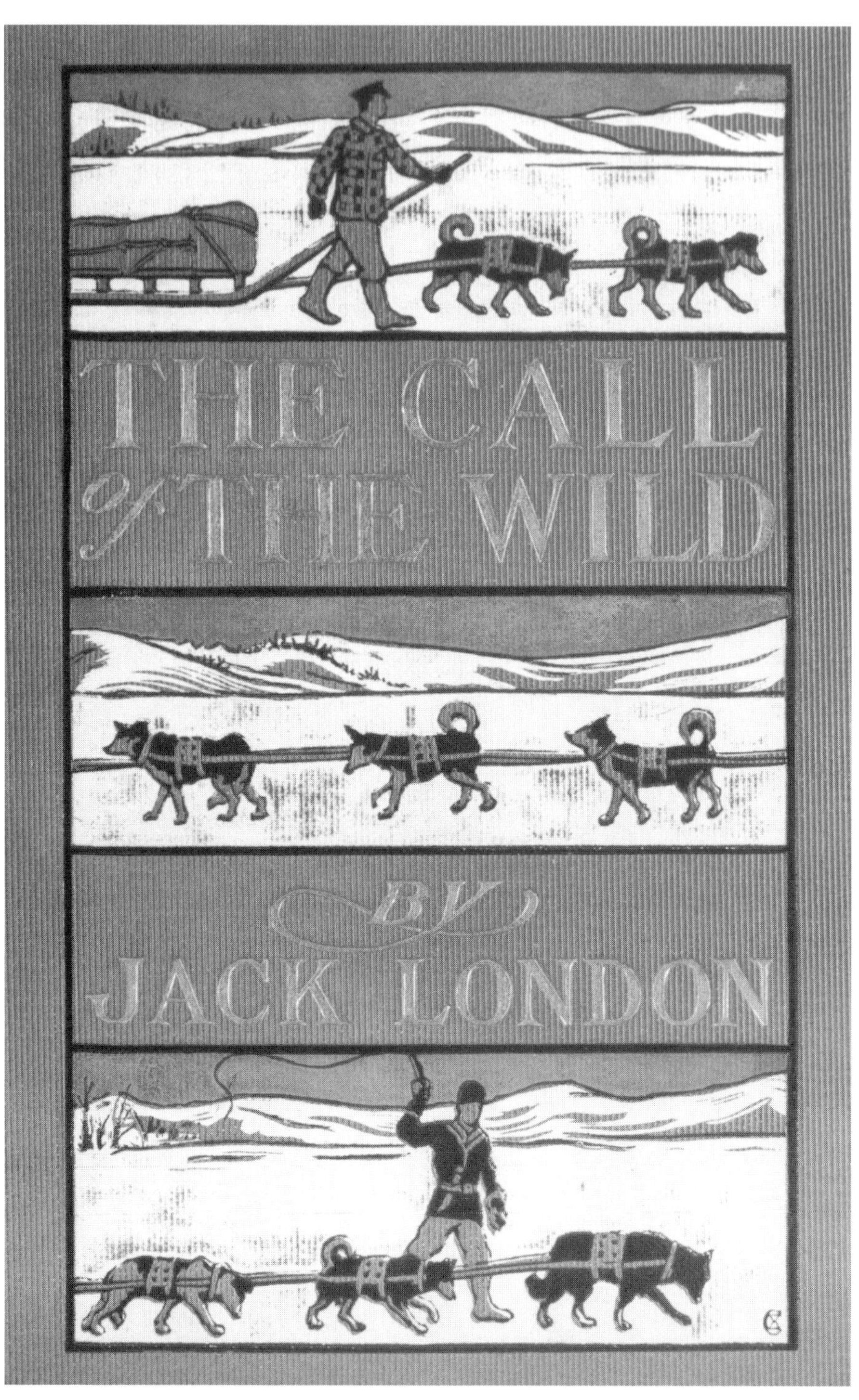

The Call of the Wild, *the story of a heroic dog, became Jack London's best-known and most loved work. London was a great lover of dogs and wrote the book—originally meant as a short story—because he felt guilty for writing about a vicious canine in an earlier story, "Bâtard."*

CHAPTER

FAME

By 1902, Jack London had established himself as a successful, up-and-coming writer. During the first few years of the century he wrote—and sold—an enormous amount of work. Much of it was set in the Northland and drew upon his memories and experiences, generously colored by his vivid imagination and his ability to shape events into simple but stirring, almost mythic, tales.

In addition to *The Son of the Wolf,* London published several dozen stories and articles in 1900. They appeared in a wide variety of the nation's newspapers and magazines and brought his name to the attention of many readers. In 1901 he published more stories and articles as well as a second book, a collection of Klondike stories called *The God of His Fathers.* The following year saw the appearance of more articles and three more books. One of them, *A Daughter of the Snows,* was London's first novel. It was also set in the Klondike. *Children of the Frost,* published the same year, was London's third volume of Northland stories, and some critics consider it his best story collection. It is noteworthy because its stories are about the Native Americans of the north, not just the white prospectors and adventurers of the region. One story often reprinted from this collection is "The Law of Life," an account of an old man who is left to die by his people and who accepts death as part of the great pattern of existence that controls all living things. Another tale, "In the Forests of the North," tells of a white man living among the American Indians and of the conflict that arises when other whites enter their community. *Children of the Frost* was a success both in the United States and in Great Britain, where reviewers praised London's sympathetic treatment of native characters and compared him to Rudyard Kipling, one of the most popular English writers of the day.

The third book that London published in 1902 was *The Cruise of the Dazzler,* a novel for young people based, at least loosely, on his adventures as an oyster pirate aboard his sloop, the *Razzle Dazzle.* An inscription that London wrote on the front page of a copy of one of his books—*Tales of the Fish Patrol,* another work for young readers, published in 1905—says much about how he did not merely report but often reshaped real-life experiences while he transformed them into literary works. "Find here," he wrote, "sometimes hinted, sometimes told, and sometimes made different, the days of my boyhood."

Not all these works were masterpieces. Neither London nor his publisher was pleased with *A Daughter of the Snows,* a novel that overflows with ideas but is populated by stiff and unrealistic characters. London later said regretfully that he had poured enough ideas for a dozen novels into this single failure. The short stories, however, were far more successful. They fed a new literary appetite in the United States—a taste for vigorous, elemental adventure tales, which seemed bold and refreshing after the sentimental, genteel stories that had dominated popular fiction for much of the late 19th century. By the time he wrote *Children of the Frost,* London was growing rather tired of writing about the Klondike, but that was what publishers wanted from him. He complained in a letter to Cloudesley Johns, "A man does one thing in a passable manner and the dear public insists upon his continuing to do it to the end of his days." Whenever his own memory and inspiration began to run dry, he scanned old newspaper articles about the gold rush and wrote to friends he had met in the Klondike, seeking story ideas.

London's personal life, as well as his professional one, changed dramatically in the years immediately after his return from the Klondike. His long infatuation with Mabel Applegarth, whom he had once hoped to marry, faded. She had not encouraged or supported his writing career as he believed she should, and he had come to feel that her ideas and values conformed too much to the ordinary conventions of middle-class society for him. They remained friends for a long time, however. London maintained lasting relationships with many people who had mattered to him. Frank Atherton, the Applegarths, Johnny Heinold, hoboes, friends from the waterfront or the Klondike—all remained part of his life, even as his growing success as a writer brought him into a new circle of literary and artistic acquaintances in the Bay Area.

In late 1899 London met Anna Strunsky, an attractive student of Russian descent who was passionately interested in socialism and the labor movement. They formed a close friendship that included much letter writing. Eventually they worked together on a novel in letter form, *The Kempton-Wace Letters* (1903), which consists of a correspondence on the nature and purpose of love: Should it be regarded as a practical, biological matter or as a romantic ideal? London declared his love for Strunsky while they were writing the book. She did not share his feelings but considered him a close friend.

London's increased income and the prospect of still greater success allowed him to improve his and his family's living conditions. In the spring of 1900 he rented a seven-room house into which he moved with Flora and Johnny.

London fell in love with his friend Anna Strunksy, a writer who was deeply interested in social issues. Although Strunsky did not fully share London's feelings, years after his death she wrote: "He was youth, adventure, romance. He was a poet and a thinker. He loved greatly and was greatly loved."

Flora London was thrilled—at last she would be mistress of a handsome home. Things could only get better now that her boy's star was rising. Sadly for Flora, however, she very soon lost her position as the woman of the house.

Bessie Maddern had been a friend of London's for some years. Their friendship had deepened after the death of London's friend and Maddern's fiancé, Fred Jacobs. The two spent much time together, bicycling and talking about books or about London's writing. On the first of April, while Maddern was helping to hang curtains in London's new house, London was seized with the impulse to propose to her. He later wrote to Strunsky: "I was rather sudden. I always do things that way."

A week later London and Maddern were married, and she moved into his house. Eliza, who still lived in Oakland, had her work cut out for her calming the spats that erupted between Flora and Bessie in the first weeks of the marriage. After a few months Jack rented a small cottage nearby for Flora and Johnny.

Many people have speculated at great length about London's reasons for marrying Maddern, whom he always claimed he did not love. Some have said that he felt sorry for her, that he wanted to start a family (he once said he wanted to sire seven sons), or that he felt that a wife would provide him with the services of a housekeeper and secretary at no cost. Others point to *The Kempton-Wace Letters,* in which London, in the persona of Herbert Wace, argued for a logical, scientific, cold-blooded approach to love and marriage. At the time he married Maddern, London had experienced two heartfelt infatuations, neither of which had worked out for him. Perhaps he truly believed that a marriage based on companionship and shared interests was preferable to the unruly and unreliable passions of the heart.

Whatever London's reasons for marrying Bessie, the marriage did not flourish. Bessie was a quiet, serious woman who resented London's habit of regularly filling their house with loud, talkative friends of both sexes who ate and drank, laughed and talked, read new stories aloud, and enjoyed games and sports for hours on end. He, in turn, resented her coldness and jealousy. Despite these stresses, however, the couple had two daughters, Joan, born in 1901, and Bess, called Becky, in 1902. By the time Becky was born, London had moved the family into a spacious redwood house in the hills above Oakland, where he continued to entertain "the Crowd," an assortment of the Bay Area's poets, artists, writers, and socialists.

Bessie Maddern London, Jack's first wife, was photographed with the couple's two daughters, Joan, on the left, and Bess, in 1905, after the couple's marriage had ended. Joan would later write about her imperfect relationship with her father in Jack London and His Daughters.

London's growing fame brought requests from periodicals for articles and stories—for example, the *San Francisco Examiner* commissioned him to write a 10-part series on a German-American club's annual 10-day shooting contest in Oakland. Clubs and societies in the area also requested him to be a speaker at their meetings. He lectured on topics ranging from "Women's Suffrage" to "The Tramp." For nearly a month in the summer of 1901, London was the special guest lecturer at an artists' retreat in Forestville, in Sonoma County, north of San Francisco. His involvement in socialism had not slackened. In 1901 the Oakland Socialist Democratic Party, realizing that Jack London was their best-known member, ran him as their candidate for mayor of Oakland. No one took his candidacy seriously—the *San Francisco Evening Post* humorously speculated that if he won he would change Oakland's name to London or Jacktown—but the affair attracted fresh publicity and may have helped sell some of his books.

In 1902 the American Press Association asked London to travel to South Africa to interview the leaders of the recently ended Boer War, which had pitted the British against the Dutch farmers, or *Boers,* who had settled parts of the region. Pleased to be regarded as a serious journalist, London agreed and headed to New York City on the first leg of the trip. When he got to New York he learned that the people he was supposed to interview had already left South Africa, making it impossible for him to complete the assignment. Instead, London convinced an editor at Macmillan, a New York City book publisher, to fund a writing project of his own.

He went to England, to live in the slums of London's East End, notoriously one of the poorest and most wretched places in Europe, and to write about what he saw there. Other writers had made themselves famous by exposing the vile conditions of slum life. In his 1849 novel *Redburn,* Herman Melville had written movingly of the misery he saw in the slums of Liverpool, England, and Jacob Riis's 1890 book of photographs, *How the Other Half Lives,* had painted a shocking portrait of urban New York. London believed that he could not only produce a powerful book, but he also could perform a vital social service by calling public attention to the sufferings that the capitalist economic and social system inflicted on the lowest of the low.

London spent most of August and part of September in the East End, among the homeless, the jobless, the hopeless, and those who had been tossed onto society's junk heap because they were too old or sick to work. Although he

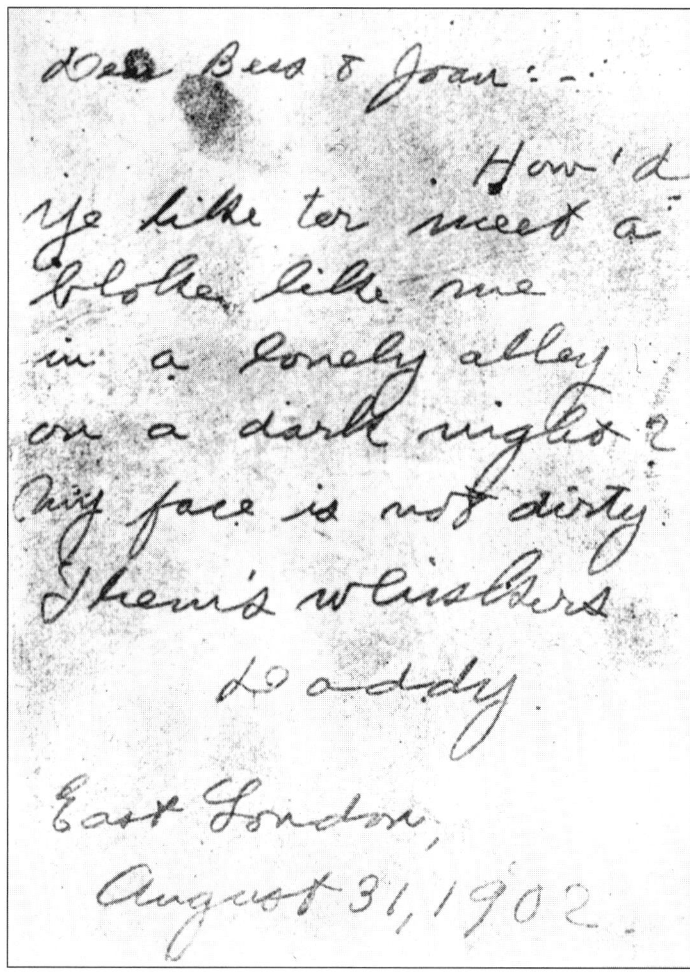
Dear Bess & Joan:—

How'd ye like ter meet a bloke like me in a lonely alley on a dark night? My face is not dirty. Them's whiskers.

Daddy

East London,
August 31, 1902.

While posing as a tramp in England's worst slums, Jack London sent this note to his family in California, along with a photograph showing him as a "bloke" in cap and whiskers.

had a comfortable room, he spent little time there except when he was writing. Disguised as an out-of-work American seaman, he often spent whole days and nights with the homeless vagabonds on the street as they moved from place to place in search of a meal or a place where the police might let them snatch a few hours' sleep. During this time London also managed to read an enormous amount of what had been published on the subject of poverty in England. When he left he carried with him dozens of black-and-white photographs that he had taken himself and a manuscript that he called *The People of the Abyss.*

After a brief trip through France, Germany, and Italy, London returned to the United States in November. He delivered *The People of the Abyss* to Macmillan. A few chapters appeared as magazine articles before the entire book was published in 1903. London would later say that he loved this sociological volume more than anything else he had written: "No other book of mine took so much of my young heart and tears as that study of the economic degradation of the poor." In the book, he wrote of how grinding poverty, humiliation, and despair turned the doomed children of the slums into "a mess of unmentionable obscenity," twisted, brutal, miserable, vicious beings who resembled "gorillas" and "apes." "If this is the best that civilization can do for the human," London concluded, "then give us howling and naked savagery."

Macmillan was also interested in new books from London, who on the first of December sat down to write what he called "an animal story." By the time it was finished in late January 1903, the story had become a short novel. The *Saturday Evening Post,* one of the country's most popular magazines, at once offered to publish it in five installments. Macmillan would then publish it in book form. London hesitated in choosing a title for the story, but he finally settled on *The Call of the Wild.* On the surface it is a simple story, the tale of a dog named Buck, raised by loving

masters on a ranch in California. A dishonest servant sells Buck, who ends up a sled dog in the Klondike, where in order to survive and adapt he must learn the rules of a challenging new existence. After his last and most loved human master dies, Buck hears the "call of the wild" that had been buried deep in his canine blood and becomes the leader of a pack of wolves.

This photo created by Jack London for The People of the Abyss *sets the scene for his firsthand survey of the plight of the poor. "I never conceived such a mass of misery in the world before," he wrote to his friend Anna Strunsky.*

When London agreed to accept a single, one-time payment from Macmillan for *The Call of the Wild,* with no possibility of earning royalties on future sales, he had no way of knowing that it would become far and away his best-selling book. Macmillan printed an extremely handsome edition of the novel and promoted it heavily. *The Call of the Wild* became an instant bestseller. Now Jack London was more than a successful writer. He was a star.

The year 1903 brought not only international fame but personal upheaval for London. His three-year marriage to Bessie, never on the strongest footing, fell apart as London fell in love with another woman, Charmian Kittredge. He had known her for a few years—in fact, he had broken a lunch date with her on April 7, 1900, to marry Bessie.

Kittredge was an attractive, athletic woman almost four years older than London. She had grown up in the house of her aunt, Ninetta Eames, a member of the Bay Area's literary community. Kittredge and London had first met in 1900 when Eames interviewed London for the *Overland Monthly*. Kittredge had then reviewed London's *The Son of the Wolf* for that periodical. In the years that followed she became a regular member of "the Crowd" of London's friends, but by early summer of 1903 her relationship with London was moving beyond friendship.

Ninetta Eames owned a property called Wake Robin Lodge in Glen Ellen, a town nestled in the Sonoma Valley. As London's friend, Eames made a rental cabin available to him. In May 1903 London took Bessie and their two young daughters there for a vacation. After a time, however, he returned to their home in Oakland to work. Two months later he finally admitted that his marriage was a sham and told Bessie that he was leaving her but that he would always see that she and the girls were provided for financially. The outraged Bessie—who thought her husband was leaving her for Anna Strunsky, with whom London had remained friendly—announced that she would never give him a divorce.

Because he was still a married man, London could not make his relationship with Charmian Kittredge public—the scandal would have damaged both of their reputations and very likely his career as well. So he moved into a new apartment in Oakland, sharing quarters with Frank Atherton and his family. He also rented a house for Flora and Johnny, for whom he still felt responsible. He and Kittredge continued to see one another privately, however. She also took on another role, one that was to become an important part of London's professional life. She acted as his personal editor and secretary, organizing his letters and contracts, keeping files of the various drafts of his work, and editing and proofreading his material as it came from the printer.

By the fall of 1903 London had also purchased a boat, a small sailboat he named *Spray,* and was enjoying sailing it around the bay. He worked onboard, and the boat was a highly suitable setting for writing, because London was now working on a novel about the sea. His new book concerned a young man who falls off a ferryboat in San Francisco Bay and is picked up by a sealing ship. The ship's captain, Wolf Larsen, refuses to put the young fellow ashore, forcing him to join the vessel's crew. When *The Sea-Wolf* was published in 1904, readers and critics responded well to its vivid descriptions of dramatic events at sea. They also responded to the fierce, larger-than-life character of the captain, whose philosophy is that only the strong survive: "The big eat the little that they may continue to move, the strong eat the weak that they may retain their strength. The lucky eat the most and survive the longest, that's all." One reviewer called the best-selling book "the novel of the year in America." Some, however, felt that the sentimental love story between the young man and a shipwrecked poetess, which occupies the second half of the book, weakened what might otherwise have been a true classic.

In 1904 London was once again invited to serve as a journalist. The Hearst Newspaper Syndicate hired him to go to Asia to report on the Russo-Japanese War. Russia and Japan were fighting over rival claims to territory in a part of northeastern China known as Manchuria, and London was eager to reach the front lines. He sailed to Yokohama, revisiting briefly the Japanese port where he had narrowly escaped getting into trouble after his sealing cruise on the *Sophia Sutherland,* and after various frustrating difficulties with the Japanese authorities he succeeded in traveling north through Korea to Manchuria. Depressed by the red tape that was keeping him from the scene of the real action, he wrote to Kittredge, "I have so far done no decent work. Have

While reporting on the Russo-Japanese War in Asia, London was photographed with Japanese soldiers. In an article for the San Francisco Examiner, *he noted the "quietness, strictness, and orderliness" of the Japanese troops and contrasted them with "our boys," American soldiers who liked to "kick up a row."*

lost enthusiasm and hardly hope to do anything decent." London did, however, enjoy the camaraderie of other war reporters, and he did produce a series of stories for the *San Francisco Examiner,* one of the Hearst papers. Many of these pieces were portraits of ordinary Asian people such as peasants and soldiers. Like the stories in *Children of the Frost,* these articles revealed London's ability to see and communicate the interest and humanity of nonwhite characters.

After a brawl with a Japanese servant who had been bullying his own servant, a Korean man named Manyoungi, London found himself in trouble with the Japanese military officials in the area. Soon afterward he set out for home, taking Manyoungi with him. Back in California the Korean would work as London's valet for the next several years.

Around this time Bessie changed her mind and decided to divorce London. She charged him with "desertion and cruelty" and named Anna Strunsky as the woman who had broken up their marriage. The gossip-hungry public devoured newspaper articles about London's private life as eagerly as it read his war reports. After London agreed to build a house for Bessie and the girls, the court awarded her a divorce in November 1904. According to the divorce laws of the time, one year from that date Jack London would be free to marry again—and this time, he was sure, he would be marrying the right woman. Charmian Kittredge, he was convinced, was his ideal "Mate Woman," as he called her, someone who combined feminine appeal, unashamed sensuality, a sharp and well-educated mind, and a love of exertion and adventure. Indeed, the relationship between the two would be happy and fulfilling for the rest of London's life.

Both London and Kittredge loved Glen Ellen and the Sonoma Valley, which the Native Americans had called the Valley of the Moon. In early 1905 London fell into a deep depression that he called the Long Sickness. His divorce, the hardships and frustrations of his Asian trip, and his growing financial responsibilities (he was almost never out of debt) were taking their toll. He went to Wake Robin Lodge, but even that beloved spot could not lift his spirits. Kittredge later recalled in *The Book of Jack London* that it was a horseback ride through the valley, on an ancient trail through magnificent redwood groves under "a great broken blue-and-white sky," that pierced London's melancholy and revived his joy in living. London decided to make Glen Ellen his home. In June he bought a parcel of ranchland there. Over the years he would add to it with six additional purchases of land, until by 1911 he owned a 1,400-acre tract of forest and field that he called Beauty Ranch. The ranch would be Jack's home throughout his 30s, although he also bought a house in Oakland for Flora, Johnny, and Jennie Prentiss to share. It had a large upstairs room for him and Kittredge to use when they visited Oakland.

Since his return from Asia, London had made frequent appearances as a lecturer, once alarming a sedate audience at the University of California in Berkeley with a fiery lecture on the topic "Revolution." He was made president of a new socialist club in San Francisco and, in 1905, once again ran unsuccessfully for mayor of Oakland as the Socialist Party candidate. By this time, however, the general public was becoming increasingly uncomfortable with socialism and anything else that seemed to threaten prosperity and the established order. London certainly expressed his scorn for capitalism as it was practiced in Europe and the United States. He had nothing but criticism for a social, political, and economic system that could permit large-scale poverty and corruption. However, he never encouraged acts of violence or lawlessness, even in the service of social change—he believed that it would be many long years before the "socialist revolution" would come about. Still, London's candidacy, along with some of his more dramatic statements—often taken out of context, as when a newspaper reported him as crying "To hell with the Constitution!"—turned many people against his politics and may even have kept some of them from buying his books. But enough people were curious about this hot-blooded, outspoken, handsome, notorious young author that audiences flocked to hear him speak.

In October 1905 London began his first and only national lecture tour in Lawrence, Kansas. For several months he kept up a hectic schedule of train travel, writing every day, and public speaking, often twice in a single day. In November, when London was free to remarry, Kittredge joined him and they were married in Chicago. The news of London's remarriage, like some of his political speeches, scandalized some audience members in the conservative Midwestern states, but people continued to crowd the auditoriums where he spoke. At the end of the year Jack and Charmian interrupted the lecture tour for a honeymoon during which they visited Jamaica and other Caribbean islands and then spent some time in Florida. After outstandingly successful

At their home in Glen Ellen, miles north of San Francisco, Jack and Charmian London were awakened before dawn by the earthquake that destroyed much of San Francisco on April 18, 1906. They rushed to the city and spent hours wandering the wrecked streets past once-familiar landmarks and watching the desperate work of firefighters. Charmian London later estimated that they covered 40 miles before falling asleep in a doorway.

appearances in New York City and at Yale University in Connecticut, London came to the end of his lecture tour in February 1906 in Grand Forks, North Dakota. The Londons were ready to start on their next big project.

Early in 1906 London notified a number of magazines and newspapers that he was planning to build a 45-foot sailboat. He and his wife would then spend up to seven years sailing it around the world. "If the whim strikes us, we'll go

text continues on page 82

SOCIALISM: AN END TO MATERIAL WANT AND WRETCHEDNESS

Jack London wrote the speech "Revolution" in 1905 and delivered it many times during a lecture tour that year and on other occasions later in his life. The speech celebrates the growth of socialism around the world and predicts a coming socialist revolution. London bitingly criticizes conditions that he found intolerable in a civilized society and envisions a world transformed by a new economic system:

And now, how fares modern man? Consider the United States, the most prosperous and enlightened country of the world. In the United States there are 10,000,000 people living in poverty. By poverty is meant that condition in life in which, through lack of food and adequate shelter, the mere standard of working efficiency cannot be maintained. In the United States there are 10,000,000 people who have not got enough to eat. In the United States, because they have not got enough to eat, there are 10,000,000 people who cannot keep the ordinary measure of strength in their bodies. This means that these 10,000,000 people are perishing, are dying, body and soul, slowly, because they have not enough to eat. All over this broad, prosperous, enlightened land, are men, women, and children who are living miserably. In all the great cities, where they are segregated in slum ghettos by hundreds of thousands and by millions, their misery becomes beastliness. No caveman ever starved as chronically as they starve, slept as vilely as they sleep, ever festered with rottenness and disease as they fester, nor ever toiled as hard and for as long hours as they toil.

...Unlike the caveman, modern man cannot get food and shelter whenever he feels like working for it. Modern man has first to find the work, and in this he is often unsuccessful. Then misery becomes acute. This acute misery is chronicled daily in the newspapers. Let several of the countless instances be cited.

In New York City lived a woman, Mary Mead. She had three children: Mary, one year old; Johanna, two years old; Alice, four years old. Her husband could find no work. They starved. They were evicted from their shelter at 160 Steuben Street. Mary Mead strangled her baby, Mary, one year old; strangled Alice, four years old; failed to strangle Johanna, two years old, and then herself took poison. Said the father to police: "Constant poverty had driven my wife insane."

. . . In a room at the Soto House, 32 Fourth Street, San Francisco, was found the body of W.G. Robbins. He had turned on the gas. Also found was his diary, from which the following extracts are made:—

March 3.—No chance of getting anything here. What will I do?

March 7.—Cannot find anything yet.

March 8.—Am living on doughnuts at five cents a day.

March 9.—My last quarter gone for room rent.

March 10.—God help me. Have only five cents left. Can get nothing to do. What next? Starvation or—? I have spent my last nickel to-night. What shall I do? Shall it be steal, beg, or die? I have never stolen, begged, or starved in all my fifty years of life, but now I am on the brink—death seems the only refuge.

March 11.—Sick all day—burning fever this afternoon. Had nothing to eat to-day or since yesterday noon. My head, my head. Good-by, all.

. . . With the natural resources of the world, the machinery already invented, a rational organization of production and distribution, and an equally rational elimination of waste, the able-bodied workers would not have to labor more than two or three hours per day to feed everybody, clothe everybody, house everybody, educate everybody, and give a fair measure of little luxuries to everybody. There would be no more material want and wretchedness, no more children toiling out their lives, no more men and women and babes living like beasts and dying like beasts. . . . The spiritual, intellectual, and artistic uplift consequent upon such a condition of society would be tremendous. All the human world would surge upward in a mighty wave.

off to a thousand different and remote places that no tourist has ever heard of," he wrote. To pay for the boat, which was to be called the *Snark* after the mysterious, elusive beast in Lewis Carroll's poem *The Hunting of the Snark,* London took on a crushing load of writing assignments and also worked hard to line up publishers in advance for the articles he planned to write during the trip.

Despite London's hard work, nothing, it seemed, could go right with the vessel from the beginning. There were countless delays and disputes with contractors and workers. In the end the boat that had been expected to cost $7,000 cost London more than four times that amount. The most disastrous delay, however, affected much more than the *Snark.* On April 18 a devastating earthquake struck San Francisco. The quake and the fires that swept through the city afterward disrupted all transport, industry, and construction in the region.

After the quake hit, Jack and Charmian wandered the rubble-strewn streets of the city, astounded by the destruction they saw all around them. Biographer Russ Kingman reports that at first London refused to write about it: "What use trying? One could only string big words together, and curse the futility of them." But he agreed to report on the quake for *Collier's* magazine, for 25 cents a word. "San Francisco is gone," he wrote. "Nothing remains of it but memories. . . . Within an hour after the earthquake shock, the smoke of San Francisco's burning was a lurid tower visible 100 miles away. And for three days and nights this lurid tower swayed in the sky, reddening the sun, darkening the day, and filling the land with smoke."

Eventually work on the *Snark* resumed. It was once again fraught with delays and problems. London was later to discover that his wife's uncle, whom he had paid to oversee the construction, had neglected many key details and allowed the builders to use shoddy materials. When London finally launched the boat in February 1907, months later than he had planned, it leaked and one engine did not work. After more delays and more expenses, though, he was ready to begin the glorious cruise in April. He said farewell to his young daughters, whom he saw infrequently but who adored him; Joan wrote later in *Jack London and His Daughters* of her heartbreak when she realized that she would not see her father again for "so long that it might as well be forever."

"It was a beautiful, bright, sunshiny day when we passed out of the Golden Gate, with hundreds of whistles tooting at us a farewell salute," wrote Martin Johnson, a young man from Kansas who had written to London offering his services on the cruise and had been hired as cook and general crewman. Also aboard were Charmian London's uncle, who proved as poor a navigator as he had been a foreman, the family's Japanese servant, and an engineer. Friends and reporters lined the docks to watch the *Snark* sail jauntily westward toward Hawaii, her first port of call. They could not see that as she set out on her great adventure she was leaking at every seam.

Charmian London and Jack London (far right) aboard the Snark, *the vessel in which they made an ill-fated but eventful voyage through the Pacific Ocean.*

CHAPTER

6

Last Adventures

Yachts usually crossed from San Francisco to Hawaii in about two weeks. When the *Snark* arrived in Hawaii after a 27-day crossing, the Londons discovered that the newspapers had already reported them lost at sea. But although the *Snark* had not sunk, it did have a host of serious problems with both structure and personnel. London dug into his pockets for major repairs to the boat. He also replaced several crewmembers, including his wife's useless uncle. Throughout the voyage, London continued to fire and replace men in a vain effort to find the perfect staff. Martin Johnson, who later became a noted explorer and travel writer, was the only one who stayed with the *Snark* to the end.

Despite these vexations, the Londons' five-month stay in Hawaii was pleasurable and productive. In Honolulu they stayed in a hotel owned by a man who had been a friend of London's in Dawson City; reminiscing about the Klondike may have inspired London to write "To Build a Fire." He completed the story during his stay in Hawaii and it went on to become, perhaps, the most famous of his short fiction. People showered the visiting celebrity with invitations and kindness, but it was London's genuine warmth and

Jack London had a robust sense of humor and was willing to appear ridiculous for the sake of fun. In addition to posing in hula attire in Hawaii, he dressed as a pirate for a masquerade ball on the island of Guadalcanal.

charm as much as his fame that won him many new friends in the islands. He even made friends on the island of Molokai, which at that time housed a well-known leper colony. Despite the warnings of acquaintances who urged them to stay away for fear of becoming infected with leprosy (which, though contagious, is not easily transmissible from person to person), the Londons visited the colony and even joined in its Fourth of July celebrations. In "The Lepers of Molokai," written for a magazine called *The Woman's Home Companion,* London movingly described his experiences there and pleaded for greater tolerance and generosity toward those who suffered the disease and the valiant doctors dedicated to helping them.

While in Hawaii the Londons traveled by horseback, always one of their favorite pastimes, through rain forests and into volcanoes. After seeing young men surfing, London was determined to try the sport, which was all but unknown in the continental United States at the time. He got knocked around by the waves at first, but after a while he was able to ride the board. Such distractions, however, did not prevent him from writing for several hours each day. He wrote a number of stories and articles and also began a novel called *Martin Eden,* which has many autobiographical elements. The story of a poor young man who overcomes enormous obstacles to become a successful writer, *Martin Eden* is regarded by some modern readers as one of London's most important works.

The *Snark* left Hawaii in October, bound for the Marquesas Islands of the South Pacific. After a voyage made difficult by an almost disastrous shortage of drinking water, the Londons reached the Marquesas, from which they sailed on to Tahiti in Polynesia. There they received mail, including bad news. London's financial affairs, which Charmian's aunt Ninetta Eames had been managing, were in a mess. Eames had changed banks without telling London, and as a result he had written several checks on an account that no longer existed. She had also been overcharging him for her services and spending his money in ways he had not authorized. The Londons left the *Snark* in Tahiti in early January 1908 and returned to California by steamship to straighten things out with Eames and raise new funds by promising work to Jack's publishers. A few weeks later they were back in Tahiti and ready to continue cruising through the South Pacific islands.

In Samoa, London delivered his "Revolution" speech at the island's biggest hotel and made a pilgrimage to the grave of Robert Louis Stevenson, the author of *Treasure*

Island and many other books, whom he much admired. Russ Kingman reports that London declared to Charmian, "I wouldn't have gone out of my way to visit the grave of any other man in the world." The *Snark* then sailed for Fiji and the Solomon Islands north of Australia. By this time conditions aboard were deteriorating. Jack suffered from the mosquito-borne illness malaria, and both he and Charmian had yaws, an infectious tropical disease characterized by ulcerating sores. London was also very worried about his grotesquely swollen hands and peeling skin, which may have been side effects of severe sunburn. He had to seek treatment for these ailments in a hospital in Sydney, Australia.

The Londons now made a painful decision. They had planned to see much of the world on their multiyear trip; the *Snark*'s engines and removable masts would have allowed London to navigate it up rivers, which he had hoped to do in China, Egypt, and Europe. Crossing the Pacific was to have been just the beginning. But Jack, weakened by disease, could no longer be an active part of the boat's crew. The adventure was over. The Londons left the *Snark* in Australia to be sold—it eventually brought $4,500—and recrossed the Pacific on a passenger ship to Ecuador in South America. They then traveled on to Oakland by way of Panama, New Orleans, and the Grand Canyon. London had given Martin Johnson enough money to complete his trip around the world. In 1913 the young man would publish *Through the South Seas with Jack London.* Together with London's own *The Cruise of the* Snark (1911) and Charmian Kittredge London's *The Log of the* Snark (1915), Johnson's book offers a detailed account of an eventful and adventurous year, some of it spent exploring islands that were still very far off the beaten tourist path. Johnson remained a lifelong friend of the Londons.

At home in Glen Ellen, London recovered his health and resumed the business of writing new material and selling what he had already written. As both author and public personality, London was constantly appearing in print in these years. Sometimes he was the subject of controversy, as when he and President Theodore Roosevelt debated in a series of published letters the accuracy of London's nature writing or when a Honolulu newspaper reported that London had engaged in a drunken saloon brawl. Still, London remained one of the nation's most popular authors. The period of his life that included the *Snark* voyage also produced some of his finest work.

White Fang, published in 1906 before the *Snark* cruise, is today London's best-known novel after *The Call of the Wild.* The two are often considered a pair, and, in fact, London planned the second novel as a "companion" to the first. Both involve dogs and Arctic settings. In *White Fang,* London sought to "reverse the process" he had illustrated in the earlier book. Instead of showing how a domestic dog could become wild, he would depict the "civilizing" of a wolf-dog hybrid, who begins as a wild animal and is savagely mistreated by one of his human captors, only to end up tame and happy on the same Santa Clara ranch from which Buck had been stolen in *The Call of the Wild.* "It should make a hit," wrote London to his editor at Macmillan as he planned the book. It did, although never as big a hit as *The Call of the Wild.* London himself, however, considered *White Fang* the better book.

Jack London felt that in Charmian, his second wife, he had found the perfect partner. She was vigorous, intelligent, and free-spirited—the perfect mate for a man like him. Throughout their marriage he called her "Mate-Woman" or "Mate," as on the title page of a copy of White Fang *that he inscribed to her.*

Before leaving Oakland on the cruise, London had written a series of articles for *Cosmopolitan* magazine about his experiences as a tramp. In 1907 these appeared in book form as *The Road*. Just before the cruise, in the midst of all the difficulties and delays he was encountering with the *Snark,* London managed to write *The Iron Heel,* which was published in 1908. Part socialist tract, part visionary science fiction, *The Iron Heel* is a difficult novel to classify, and it perplexed many readers. "It was a labor of love," London wrote in a letter, "and a dead failure as a book. The book-buying public would have nothing to do with it, and I got nothing but knocks from the Socialists."

London presents the novel as a manuscript written by Avis Everhard, the widow of Ernest Everhard (London used his Michigan cousin's name), who was portrayed as the leader of a failed socialist movement of the early 20th century. The manuscript describes a ruthless, oppressive government that Everhard calls the Iron Heel, a tyranny that crushes all dissent and places wealth and power in the hands of a few. After this government brutally quells a violent revolt by the impoverished masses of the Chicago slums, Everhard is killed trying to organize a revolution in the name of liberty. His widow's manuscript is edited some seven centuries later by a professor who points out that the Iron Heel government continued in power for three centuries after Everhard's death before a more peaceful and egalitarian socialist society, the Brotherhood of Man, emerged. It was this notion—that socialism would only come into being after the capitalist system had run its full course—that so angered some socialists when *The Iron Heel* appeared.

To London's disappointment, his next novel, the autobiographical *Martin Eden,* fared no better when it was published in 1909. Reviewers responded negatively to London's portrait of a self-made literary celebrity who sees through the trappings of success to the essential emptiness of his life and then, lacking any belief in or commitment to anything outside himself, commits suicide by throwing himself into the sea.

These critical setbacks did not discourage London, who continued to write and sell as much as ever. He had to—he was perpetually in debt and had to write his 1,000 words a day just to keep money coming in to pay his bills. His correspondence from this period is filled with troublesome details about money: requests to his publishers for advances, quarrels with the newly established movie companies over the rights to film his stories, and the endless stream of expenses for his own household, including his daughters, his mother, and others such as Jennie Prentiss who depended upon him. London had not lost his love for the creative process, but being a word-machine was wearing him out. "I am so tired of writing that I would cut off my fingers and toes in order to avoid writing," he confessed in 1913 in a letter to an aspiring writer. Weary of repeating himself, aware that he sometimes wasted his energy and talent on mere potboilers (inferior works produced just for money), and running dry on inspiration, London occasionally bought plot ideas from Sinclair Lewis, a young writer who would later achieve fame in his own right and become the first American to win the Nobel Prize for literature.

London hoped to make a fortune from film versions of his books, and he even offered to star in movie adaptations. Although he had little income from the movie rights to his work, London was pleased with a 1913 version of *The Sea-Wolf* that starred the silent film star Hobart Bosworth and in which he had a part as a sailor. That same year a silent movie based on *John Barleycorn* became a Hollywood success.

Magazine and newspaper publishers continued to seek out Jack London's services as a journalist to cover all sorts of events. Many of his commissioned articles concerned boxing matches. London had long been fascinated with boxing; he enjoyed sparring (his wife, who liked all kinds of athletic activity, was frequently his sparring partner) and also loved attending boxing matches. Two of his books—*The Game* (1905) and *The Abysmal Brute* (1913)—centered on boxers and boxing. London had been reporting on matches since 1901, and after his return from the *Snark* cruise he continued to do so. In 1910 he wrote an article for the *Pittsburgh Labor Tribune* that explained why people love the "great sport" of boxing:

> It is as deep as our consciousness, and it is woven into the fibers of our being. . . . This is the ape and the tiger in us, granted. But, like the men in jail, it is in us, isn't it? We can't get away from it. . . . We like fighting. It's our nature.

Yet London pulled no punches when describing the brutality of the sport and the damage it inflicted. Years later champion boxer Gene Tunney quit boxing after reading *The Game,* and he gave a copy of the book to fellow boxer Rocky Marciano, the heavyweight champion in the early 1950s, advising him to give it a close and careful reading.

London's final big assignment as a journalist came in 1914, when *Collier's* offered him $1,000 a week—a very

After the publication of London's boxing tale The Game, *this cartoon spoofed the author, suggesting that London knew as much about "the war between the sexes" as about boxing. Colorful, attractive, and recognizable, London was the subject of scores of cartoons during his career.*

large sum at that time—to report on the situation in Mexico, which was in the middle of a long and bloody civil war and which also appeared to be on the verge of war with the United States. A conflict between U.S. sailors and Mexican authorities had escalated into a two-day attack by U.S. ships on the port of Veracruz. London went to Veracruz but found, as with the Boer and Russo-Japanese wars, that his assignment had evaporated. The tension between Mexico and the United States was ebbing. Still, Jack and Charmian spent a month in Mexico, sightseeing and visiting with some of the war reporters that he had met while covering the Russo-Japanese War.

London wrote several lengthy articles about the tense political situation in Mexico. His observations had convinced him that many of the Mexicans who claimed to be "revolutionaries" were little more than glorified bandits. This opinion, and his statement that many of the Mexican people were tired of the civil war, offended many American socialists, who accused London of selling out to big business and big government. London considered himself a true socialist to the end of his days, but his relations with the Socialist Party went downhill after the Mexico trip. In 1916 both he and his wife resigned from the party.

London also occupied himself with projects on both water and land. In 1910 he bought a 30-foot sailboat that he called the *Roamer.* This time he planned no ambitious circumnavigations—he merely wanted a boat, a successor to the *Razzle Dazzle* and the *Spray,* in which he could sail around the bay and up the Sacramento and San Joaquin rivers that flowed into it. He read, wrote, and entertained friends aboard the *Roamer,* on which the Londons sometimes stayed for a month or more at a time. Their last long cruise aboard the boat would span the period from September 1914 to January 1915.

However, London's greatest passion in the latter half of his 30s was probably his ranch. Before 1911 the Londons stayed at Wake Robin Lodge when they were in Glen Ellen, because there was no house on the ranch. The parcel of land that Jack bought in 1911, however, contained a cottage into which he and Charmian moved. Guests and workers occupied rooms in a carriage house. One of these workers was Jack's stepsister Eliza, whom he had hired to supervise the ranch while he was traveling aboard the *Snark*. She had separated from her husband but remained Jack's loyal friend and helper.

Even before the voyage London had spoken of his plan to build a large house on the ranch property. He knew exactly what he wanted—a house of mountain stone and sturdy redwood timber that would stand for a thousand years. London hired an architect to draw plans for this structure, which he called Wolf House. It would be built on four levels, with a swimming pool, a huge library, a dining room big enough for 50 people, space for the collections of artifacts the Londons would bring home from the South Seas, guest rooms, offices for Jack and Charmian, and an open-air "sleeping tower" where Jack could sleep under the stars when he felt like it. Jack and Charmian may have dreamed of raising a family at Wolf House, too, but those dreams remained out of reach. In 1910, Charmian had given birth to a daughter who lived less than two days. And in 1912 she suffered a miscarriage, ending forever the couple's hopes for children.

Construction of London's dream house began in 1911. Like the *Snark,* Wolf House ended up costing London much more than he had expected: the total bill was around $40,000. By August 1913 it was almost ready for the Londons to move in. The workmen's remaining task was to polish the floors and other woodwork with linseed oil. On the night of August 22, Charmian woke to find Eliza and Jack staring at the sky north of the cottage, where smoke and flame streamed into the sky. Wolf House was ablaze. Before anything could be done, everything but the stone

walls had been destroyed. To the end of his life, London believed that the fire had been set deliberately, perhaps by socialists who thought it was a betrayal of his ideals for him to build a "castle." The construction superintendent, however, thought that the fire was the result of spontaneous combustion in a pile of oily rags that had carelessly been left in the house. An investigation by expert researchers in 1995 concluded that the latter explanation was almost certainly the correct one.

One of the joys of London's last years was his ranch, where he ordered the construction of a stone structure that could house 300 pigs. Some laughed at the idea of a "Pig Palace," but London believed that all domesticated animals should live in clean, comfortable quarters.

Whatever the reason for the fire, London never tried to rebuild Wolf House. Instead he focused on improving the cottage with additions such as a library. He also concentrated on the business and art of farming. He threw himself full-strength into country life, hoping to make Beauty Ranch the model of a self-contained agrarian community. His ideas about agriculture and raising livestock blended a deep love of the land with an attraction to modern, scientific ideas; he drew upon sources of information as diverse as ancient Chinese manuscripts about plowing and up-to-the-minute periodicals about stock-breeding. London's interests on the ranch included blacksmithing; breeding large Shire horses imported from England; raising pigs in "the Pig Palace," a special structure that he designed himself; growing a type of spineless cactus developed by plant scientist Luther Burbank for use as cattle feed; and planting fast-growing eucalyptus trees as a source of timber.

As much as he loved the ranch, Jack still loved to travel. In the summer of 1911 he and Charmian, along with a Japanese valet named Nakata, whom they had hired in Hawaii in 1907 and who had accompanied them for part of the *Snark* voyage, took a three-month trip through northern California and part of Oregon. They preferred traveling by horseback to riding in an automobile, but they wanted to carry books and a typewriter with them, so they decided to make the journey in a wagon drawn by four horses. The trip carried them through varied landscapes and drew plenty of attention, especially when London delivered lectures along the way.

A trip in 1912 proved more daunting. The Londons and Nataka signed on as crew members aboard the *Dirigo,* a cargo freighter that was sailing from Baltimore to Seattle. The Panama Canal was not yet open to traffic—this voyage would be around the Horn, the southernmost tip of South America, through some of the coldest and roughest waters on earth. The trip lasted for nearly five months, all of it on the open sea. Although London later drew upon this experience in his novel *The Mutiny of the Elsinore,* during the voyage he was working on another book, *The Valley of the Moon.* This book concerns a young working-class couple from Oakland who struggle to survive in the dismal conditions of urban industry and eventually migrate to Glen Ellen and adopt a rural lifestyle. Upon its publication in 1913, the book was well received by both readers and many critics, who rightly saw in it many elements of London's own life.

John Barleycorn, presented as "a straight, true narrative of my personal experiences," also appeared in 1913. It was a huge hit, appealing to an audience ever eager for details about London's colorful life. London wrote the book as a plea for a ban on alcohol. Although he no longer drank as much or as often as he had in his youth, he had never really been able to control completely his desire for alcohol. Occasionally his drinking placed stress on his marriage or caused a public scene. Just before the voyage of the *Dirigo,* for example, Jack had embarked on a major drinking bout that caused a serious rift between him and Charmian. He promised to give up drinking after that. Still, he did drink after returning to California, although most people who knew London well and saw him regularly during the later part of his life claimed that they never saw him drunk. By this time, however, London was suffering from a serious illness called uremia, progressive failure of the kidneys. It is likely that drinking had contributed to, if not caused, this condition, for which there was no cure.

London knew in 1913 that he had uremia. The doctors said that he could not expect to live a long life. But London discovered from reading medical texts that men had been known to survive for 30 years with uremia. He was strong, and he was convinced that he could do even better. London kept the news of his illness from the public and determined to live as long and as well as possible. He continued to work hard, and he also traveled to Mexico in 1914. In early 1915 he and his wife went to their beloved Hawaii, where they spent five months working, swimming, sailing, riding, and visiting friends. In December of that same year they went back to Hawaii. This time, however, London was tired and weak, scarcely able to take part in the activities he had enjoyed a short time earlier. When the Londons left Hawaii in July 1916, London may have hoped to return once again to the sweet-scented, hospitable islands he loved, but he never did.

In late 1916 London's sickness was advancing, but he had reasons for optimism as well. He was still selling everything he wrote, and his income had risen to the point where he could foresee escaping the burden of debt within a few years. He had recently freed himself from the Socialist Party and no longer felt that he had to be a spokesman for anyone's cause or philosophy—he felt free to explore new ideas and new subjects in his work. *The Scarlet Plague* and *The Star Rover,* both published in book form in 1915 (*The Star Rover* first appeared as a monthly magazine serial) marked a move into new territory: the world of fantasy and science fiction. And in June 1916 London had begun reading the works of the Swiss psychologist and philosopher Carl Jung. Jung's ideas gave Jack such a welcome jolt of inspiration and intellectual excitement that, according to biographer Russ Kingman, he said to Charmian, "I tell you I am standing on the edge of a world so new, so terrible, so wonderful that I am almost afraid to look into it."

In reality, though, London was near death. He called death the "noseless one"—the grinning skull who comes for every man in the end. London could feel its presence hovering near, and he frequently experienced attacks of excruciating pain. Like many people in those days, he medicated himself with morphine to ease the pain; this was a legal and common practice at the time.

On the morning of November 22, Eliza and Charmian found Jack in his bed, apparently suffering from some sort of poisoning. They could not wake him. Two doctors arrived; one diagnosed morphine poisoning, the other kidney failure. London died later that day without regaining consciousness.

text continues on page 101

Escaping to Past Lives

In The Star Rover, *London created a character who, while imprisoned in California for murder, endured dreadful abuse and torture at the hands of his jailers. To escape the pain, he learned the trick of sending his spirit out of his body and reliving earlier existences in other eras—as a Viking, a French courtier, or a pioneer boy in the American West. In the novel's opening passage, inmate Darrell Standing tells how even before his imprisonment he had felt faint connections to past lives, even to the unthinkably remote origins of human life itself.*

All my life I have had an awareness of other times and places. I have been aware of other persons in me. Oh, and trust me, so have you, my reader that is to be. Read back into your childhood, and this sense of awareness I speak of will be remembered as an experience of your childhood. You were then not fixed, not crystallized. You were plastic, a soul in flux, a consciousness and an identity in the process of forming—ay, of forming and forgetting.

You have forgotten much, my reader, and yet, as you read these lines, you remember dimly the hazy vistas of other times and places into which your child eyes peered. They seem dreams to you today. Yet, if they were dreams, dreamed then, whence the substance of them? Our dreams are grotesquely compounded of the things we know. The stuff of our sheerest dreams is the stuff of our experiences. As a child, a wee child, you dreamed you fell great heights; you dreamed you flew through the air as things of the air fly; you were vexed by crawling spiders and many-legged creatures of the slime; you heard other voices, saw other faces nightmarishly familiar, and gazed upon sunrises and sunsets other than you know now, looking back, you ever looked upon.

Very well. These child glimpses are of other-worldness, of other-lifeness, of things that you had never seen in this particular world of your particular life. Then whence? Other lives? Other worlds? Perhaps, when you have read all that I shall write, you will have received answers to the perplexities I have propounded to you, and that you yourself, ere you came to read me, propounded to yourself. . . .

As for myself, at the beginnings of my vocabulary, at so tender a period that I still made hunger noises and sleep noises, yet even then did I know that I had been a star rover. Yes I, whose lips had never lisped the word "king," remembered that I had once been the son of a king. More—I remembered that once I had been a slave and a son of a slave, and worn an iron collar around my neck. . . .

Silly, isn't it? But remember, my reader, whom I hope to have travel far with me through time and space—remember, please, my reader, that I have thought much on these matters that through bloody nights and sweats of dark that lasted years long I have been alone with my many selves to consult and contemplate my many selves. I have gone through the hells of all existences to bring you news which you will share with me in a casual, comfortable hour over my printed page.

So to return I say, during the ages of three and four and five, I was not yet I. I was merely becoming as I took form in the mold of my body, and all the mighty, indestructible past wrought in the mixture of me to determine what the form of that becoming would be. It was not my voice that cried out in the night in fear of things known, which I, forsooth, did not and could not know. The same with my childish angers, my loves and my laughters. Other voices screamed through my voice, the voices of men and women aforetime, of all shadowy hosts of progenitors. And the snarl of my anger was blended with the snarls of beasts more ancient than the mountains, and the vocal madness of my child hysteria, with all the red of its wrath, was chorded with the insensate, stupid cries of beasts pre-Adamic and pregeologic in time.

Although some people speculated that he had committed suicide, there is no evidence to support this theory. London was planning a visit with his daughters a few days later and a business trip to New York soon after that; it is unlikely that he would have discussed these plans so freely during the day and then killed himself that night. Although he may have taken morphine as a painkiller and perhaps even miscalculated the dosage, the real cause of his death was the deadly kidney disease that had been eating away at him for years.

Jack London's journey through life ended less than two months short of his 41st birthday. According to his wishes he was cremated in Oakland, and friends buried his ashes in Glen Ellen, with a stone from Wolf House to mark the spot. Russ Kingman reports that years earlier, upon hearing of Fred Jacobs's death, London had said to Ted Applegarth, "He solved the mystery a little sooner." Now London had gone into that same mystery. And many who knew him felt that no words made a more fitting epitaph than those he had once written in an essay called "The Human Drift": "Behold, I have lived!"

The 1943 movie The Story of Jack *London featured Susan Hayward as Charmian and Michael O'Shea as Jack. An example of the romantic view of London's life that became part of his legacy, the movie is inaccurate and focuses on London's early adulthood and his career as a war correspondent.*

CHAPTER

7

LONDON'S LITERARY LEGACY

Jack London's literary career did not end with his death. The last of his books that he lived to see published was *The Little Lady of the Big House,* a novel about a cultured couple who establish a scientific ranch but whose marriage is sterile and tragic. Although London thought that the book would be "what I have been working toward all my writing life... a cleancut gem... a work of artistry," it is in fact one of his worst books, marred by the same stiff and melodramatic sentiments and characters that some felt had ruined the second half of *The Sea-Wolf.* In addition, many critics have made the mistake of reading *Little Lady* as Jack's own pessimistic evaluation of his life at Beauty Ranch and his marriage to Charmian, but this interpretation contradicts a tremendous amount of evidence that he never lost his enthusiasm for either his farm or his wife.

After London's death publishers continued to release the many stories, articles, and novels that he had written in his final years, including a number of South Seas stories. In the final years of his career, beginning with the *Snark* voyage, London had found a new source of inspiration in the settings and characters of Hawaii and the South Pacific islands. *South Sea Tales* (1911), his first collection of stories set in this part of the world, included "Mauki," a portrait of an islander sold into slavery who eventually regains his freedom. Mauki's revenge on a white man who had cruelly mistreated him is to take the man's head as a trophy. *A Son of the Sun* (1912) contains more South Pacific tales. In colorful prose, London painted vivid pictures of a part of the world that still seemed to him to be as exotic and untamed as the Arctic. As in some of his Northland tales, many of the South Pacific stories deal with survival in a hostile environment and with encounters between whites and natives.

Some of the best South Pacific stories appear in two collections published after London's death. The title story of *The Red One* (1918) tells of a scientist pursued by headhunters on the island of Guadalcanal who hears a mysterious, beautiful sound and discovers that it comes from something that the natives worship as a god. The scientist realizes that the object is a craft or artifact from another civilization somewhere out in space, but he knows that he will never be able to leave the island, and therefore the outside world will never know of his remarkable find. *On the Makaloa Mat* (1918) contains "The Water Baby," the last story London completed before his death. In the form of a conversation between two fishermen, the story explores some aspects of Polynesian and Christian myths, as well as such topics as waking and dreaming. It reflects London's interest in Jung, who wrote about the creative importance of mythology and dreams.

Also published after London's death were two novels about dogs, *Jerry of the Islands* (1917) and its sequel *Michael, Brother of Jerry* (1917). They were inspired by Peggy, a terrier belonging to Charmian who had accompanied the Londons on the *Snark* and died during the voyage. *Hearts of Three* (1920) was based on a movie of the same title that someone else had written and produced; *Cosmopolitan* had paid London the impressive sum of $25,000 to put it into novel

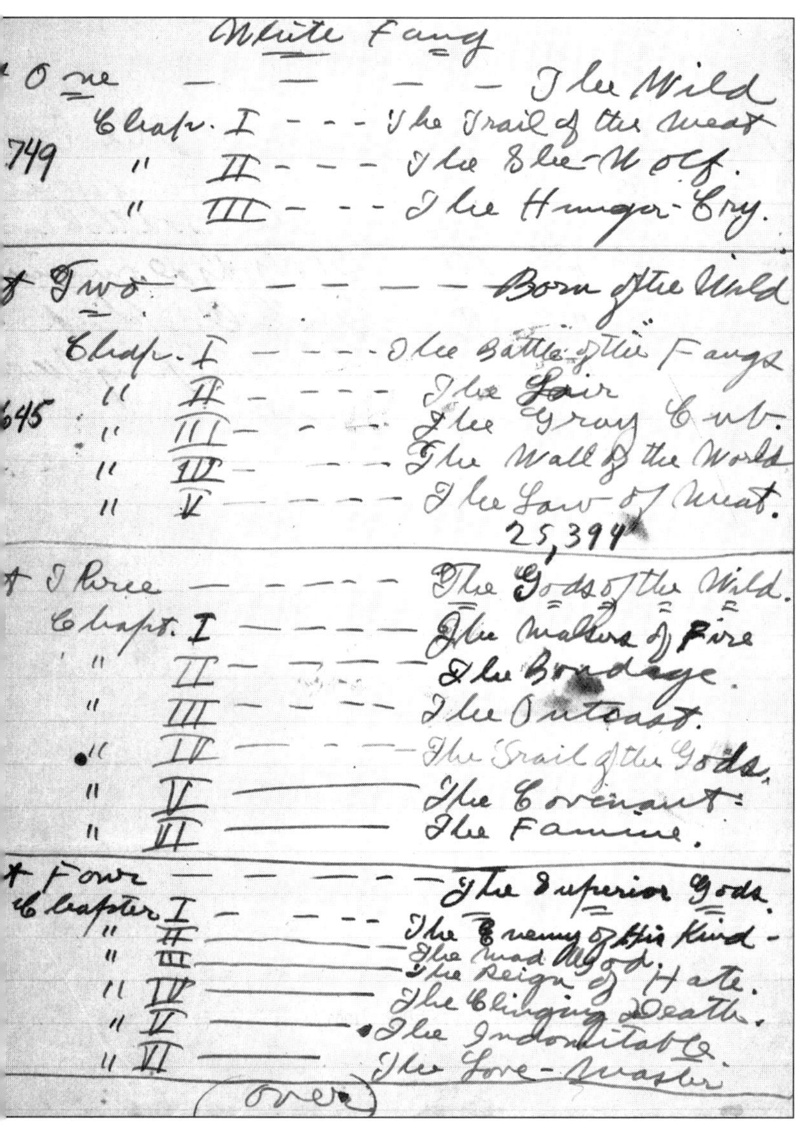

White Fang
One — The Wild
Chap. I — The Trail of the Meat
749 " II — The She-Wolf.
" III — The Hunger-Cry.

Two — Born of the Wild
Chap. I — The Battle of the Fangs
" II — The Lair
645 " III — The Gray Cub.
" IV — The Wall of the World
" V — The Law of Meat.
25,394

Three — The Gods of the Wild.
Chapt. I — The Makers of Fire
" II — The Bondage.
" III — The Outcast.
" IV — The Trail of the Gods.
" V — The Covenant.
" VI — The Famine.

Four — The Superior Gods.
Chapter I — The Enemy of His Kind -
" II — The Mad God.
" III — The Reign of Hate.
" IV — The Clinging Death.
" V — The Indomitable.
" VI — The Love-Master
(over)

London wrote this outline for White Fang, *the book he created as a companion volume to* The Call of the Wild. *Many of London's notes, letters, and other papers have been preserved in manuscript collections and are an invaluable resource for scholars who have, since the 1960s, taken a renewed critical interest in London's writing.*

form. *Dutch Courage* first published in 1922, was a collection of stories for young readers. London had also left unfinished a manuscript called *The Assassination Bureau, Ltd.* The manuscript was based on one of the ideas he had purchased from Sinclair Lewis. The novel remained unpublished until mystery writer Robert Fish completed it in 1963.

For many years after his death, London's life—with both virtues and vices exaggerated to larger-than-life proportions—in some ways overshadowed his work. As literary fashions changed, critics and scholars began to dismiss London as a crude, boisterous writer of mere popular entertainments, the author of a few "dog stories," not someone to be taken seriously as a literary figure. That began to change in 1965 with the publication of some of London's letters by scholars who had begun to reexamine his life and his place in literature. Soon a revival of London studies was underway in colleges and universities around the United States and the world (London was always an international author; he had never gone out of style in Russia, for example). London newsletters, journals, and study groups sprang up. Eventually Stanford University Press published all of London's letters in three volumes, as well as another three-volume set of his collected short stories. His articles and lectures, too, received new attention, and new biographies explored such aspects of his life as his medical history, political beliefs, and relationship with his family. Earle Labor's *Jack London,* published in 1974 and revised in 1994 with Jeanne Campbell Reesman, played a crucial role in placing London's body of work in the context of American literature. London has come to be seen as a writer whose output was wildly uneven but whose best work was powerful and visionary, shaped by a mind that was passionately engaged with big ideas, and embodied in finely crafted prose.

Some of the new attention to Jack London has highlighted troublesome aspects of his work. London's attitudes about race, for example, can be distasteful to modern readers, although they were typical of many educated people in his own time. While his personal relations with people from all backgrounds were noticeably free of racial prejudice, London did believe that there are inborn differences among the races. He thought that white Anglo-Saxons or northern Europeans were more fully evolved than other groups and would eventually prove their superiority by dominating the entire world; it was their responsibility to treat other peoples well.

Another cloud that hung over London's work was the question of plagiarism, or stealing the work of other writers. This issue arose more than once during London's lifetime, although no lawsuit was ever filed against him. When *The Call of the Wild* was published, for example, a writer named Egerton Young complained that London had stolen material from his nonfiction book *My Dogs in the Northland.* London freely admitted that he had used material from the book, just he might use information from a newspaper article or another reference source. In *The Iron Heel,* he copied word-for-word part of an article that writer Frank Harris had published in a British magazine; London claimed that he had seen the passage in a newspaper and thought it was a speech delivered publicly by the Bishop of London and therefore was a source that he could use.

More than once London admitted how hard it was for him to come up with plots and story ideas. He felt that any idea was fair game as long as he "elaborated" it into his own story, and he wove his plots from ideas gathered from newspaper and magazine articles, friends' suggestions, and even other writers' stories. As researcher Russ Kingman pointed out in *A Pictorial Life of Jack London,* London was not the only writer who resorted to such practices. London's story "Moon-Face," published in *The Argonaut* magazine, featured as one of its plot elements a dog carrying a stick of dynamite. The same month, *Century* magazine published "The Passing of Cock-Eye Blacklock," by Frank Norris, another well-known writer of the period, which contained the same situation. Both men, it appears, had borrowed the idea from a story that had appeared in *Black Cat* magazine the previous year—and that story in turn had imitated an even earlier one. Such "borrowing" was fairly common among popular writers at the time. The word-for-word copying of another writer's work, however, was and is a

7 50
mty

Jack London
Glen Ellen
Sonoma Co., Calif.

August-2-1906-

To the Editor of SEATTLE POST-INTELLIGENCER,

Dear sir:-

I have just noticed, in the POST-INTELLIGENCER for Saturday, July 28, the discrediting of my story THE UNEXPECTED, published in August McCLURE'S--------or rather, the discrediting of the statement made that the story had a foundation in fact.

If you will turn to your file of THE SAN FRANCISCO EXAMINER for October 14, 1900, you will there find an account of the double-murder committed by Michael Dennin, and of his hanging by Mrs.Nelson and her husband, Hans. I quote from that article the following:

"The United States Court, before whom Mrs.Nelson and Hans laid the whole matter of the crime and execution of Michael Dennin, has decided that the hanging of the murderer was a judicial execution."

Of course, this was news from a newspaper, and the quotation I have just made is made from the columns of a newspaper. Now, if no hanging occurred at Latuya Bay in the winter of 1899, then the whole story as published in THE EXAMINER, with many of the thumb-marks of verity, is all a newspaper lie written by newspaper men. In which case, it 's up to you, not to lambaste me, as you have done, but to turn loose and lambaste your fellow-newspaper-men who are responsible for this.

Very truly yours,

Jack London

serious matter, both illegal and unprofessional. London apologized for doing so in several cases, but he refused to apologize for using ideas and situations he encountered in other writers' work.

London has often been described as a "rugged individualist" whose life and work illustrate his belief that each person must stand alone and determine his or her own morality and destiny. This view is only partly accurate. Throughout his immensely productive 17-year writing career, London struggled to express his ideas about individualism and society. In Wolf Larsen, the hero of *The Sea-Wolf,* and Martin Eden he created perfect examples of rugged individualists. London undoubtedly felt the powerful attraction of individualism—these strong and self-contained men are among his most vivid and memorable creations. Yet each is ultimately doomed by his individualism, which makes him a lonely outcast. London believed that individuals need connections to society, to other people, to what he called "the whole human collective need." He intended Martin Eden, "who lived only for himself, fought only for himself, and, if you please, died only for himself," as a symbol of the failure of individualism carried to extremes. London himself felt linked to "the whole human collective" by his efforts to publicize the plight of the poor and by his progressive political thinking and writing. On the more personal level, his life was a study in generosity and sociability, hardly the traits of Wolf Larsen.

London's novel *Burning Daylight,* published in 1910, also criticizes individualism. The novel, which was very popular, is the story of a strong and successful Klondike adventurer who believed that "he could achieve more than other men, win out where they failed, ride to success where they perished." When he tries to conquer the big-business world of Wall Street in the same way that he had conquered the Northland, however, he is tricked out of a vast fortune. He seeks revenge against the businessmen who wronged

Several times in his career London defended himself against accusations of making up stories that he passed off as true. In 1906, the Seattle Post-Intelligencer *said that the events London had described in his story "The Unexpected" were not based on fact, as he had claimed. London wrote to the paper's editors and cleverly pointed out that if the story were indeed false, the blame lay with newspapermen and not with him.*

him, but only when he abandons his quest for wealth and power does he win what really matters—love and a happy life with his beloved in the Sonoma Valley.

Much of London's work dealt with themes that are distinctively American. One of these themes is the ideal of the "self-made man": the idea that people have the ability to create or re-create themselves, to start over, to adapt and change and grow. Another is the notion of the healing and transforming power of nature and wilderness, the belief that living off the land or returning to the natural world—especially a frontier such as the Arctic, the sea, or a remote island—can set the stage for spiritual redemption or salvation. London also explores the dark and misleading aspects of what his biographer Earle Labor calls "the American Dream and the Myth of Success," reflected in widespread popular images of shoeshine boys rising to be bank presidents and humble folk finding happiness in material goods.

In recent years London has received recognition as a pioneer in several genres, or categories, of fiction. *The Iron Heel,* which foresaw the rise of the oppressive, dictatorial type of political system known as fascism, has many weaknesses as a story. But it is a compelling example of dystopian fiction, which presents a view of a world gone horribly wrong. It probably influenced George Orwell in the writing of the much better-known dystopian novel *Nineteen Eighty-Four.*

The Scarlet Plague belongs to the subcategory of science fiction that some have called apocalyptic because it deals with an apocalypse—an event that destroys the world, or at least civilization. In London's novel, that event is a dreadful plague that appears in 2013 and kills most of the earth's population. Of those that remain, a delicate young woman from a privileged background is forced to mate with a crude servant who is little better than a caveman, while an educated professor is left to brood over the disappearance of civilization, swept away like "so much foam." The novel's lushly poetic conclusion presents an image of sea lions, wild horses, mountain lions, and wolves reclaiming California while an "old man and boy, skin-clad and barbaric," are part of the few who are beginning the long process of starting over.

One of London's strangest and most ambitious books was the fantasy he called *The Star Rover.* London based it on the story of a real ex-convict named Ed Morrell, who had been imprisoned at San Quentin and undergone long periods of painful punishment in a straitjacket. Morrell claimed that he had escaped the pain by hypnotizing himself until his spirit left his body; he said that he then "projected" his spirit across space and time. After meeting Morrell in 1912 and hearing of his experiences, which probably revived London's own outrage over his long-before treatment in New York State, London planned a novel that would be "a staggering punch against the whole damnable, rotten American Jail System." *The Star Rover,* which London hoped would be "my masterpiece," is indeed a powerful exposé of the brutal prison system, but it is also a hymn to the triumphant human spirit and its unconquerable will to survive. Its real fascination, however, lies in the episodes in which the imprisoned inmate's soul revisits its former lives as a French count, a pioneer in the American West, a Viking captured by Roman soldiers, a castaway on a deserted island, and more.

Throughout his career, London wrote about writing, in letters, essays, and fiction. From "On the Writer's Philosophy of Life" (1899) to "Eight Factors of Literary Success," published in 1917 after his death, he offered opinions and advice about the craft and business of writing, often illustrating his points with information about his own career and writing habits. But his richest picture of the writer's life occurs in *Martin Eden,* in the chapters that portray a young man's struggles to educate himself and break into the world of publishing. The book's theme is growth through greater and greater levels of awareness and insight. Its basic irony is the high cost of knowledge: Martin is a contented sailor until he begins to dream of "higher" things, but when he actually achieves the glowing dream of rags-to-riches success, he finds it ultimately worthless.

Of all his works, London will probably always be best remembered for what Labor has called "the Northland Saga," his body of stories and novels set in the Arctic. The Northland Saga brought London his most notable early successes, including *The Call of the Wild,* his real masterpiece. The finest of these works—stories such as "In a Far Country," which tells of two men who spend the winter in a remote cabin and end by killing one another, and "To the Man on the Trail," which features a surprising plot twist that illustrates the "code" by which honorable men live—are more than mere tales. Simple, powerful, symbolic, and profoundly moral, they are as unforgettable and timeless as myths or sagas.

CHRONOLOGY

1876
Born January 12 in San Francisco to Flora Wellman; in September Wellman marries John London

1879–1885
London family moves from Oakland, California, to a farm in Alameda County, California, and back to Oakland

1891
Graduates from Cole Elementary School in Oakland; buys the sloop *Razzle Dazzle* and becomes oyster pirate

1893
Takes Pacific Ocean voyage on sealing ship; first story, "Story of a Typhoon off the Coast of Japan," is published

1894
Travels with the "Army of the Unemployed"; imprisoned for vagrancy in Niagara Falls, New York

1895
Attends Oakland High School and publishes stories in the school newspaper

1896
Joins the Socialist Labor Party; enters University of California at Berkeley

1897
Arrested in February for making a public speech in Oakland

1897–98
Travels to the Yukon and Alaska on gold-prospecting trip

1899
Sells first story to *The Black Cat* magazine

1900
Marries Bessie Maddern; *The Son of the Wolf* is published

1901
Daughter Joan is born

1902
Daughter Bess ("Becky") is born; *The Cruise of the Dazzler* and *A Daughter of the Snows* are published

1903
Separates from Bessie; *The Call of the Wild* is published

1904
Travels to Japan, Korea, and Manchuria as war correspondent; divorces Bessie; *The Sea-Wolf* is published

1905
Purchases first portion of ranch in Sonoma Valley; begins national lecture tour; marries Charmian Kittredge

1906
White Fang is published

1907–8
The Road and *The Iron Heel* are published

1907–9
Sails to Hawaii and the South Sea Islands on the *Snark;* returns to California by way of South America

1909
Martin Eden is published

1910
Newborn daughter dies

1911
The Cruise of the Snark and *South Sea Tales* are published

1911–13
Wolf House is built and lost in a fire

1912
Voyages with the *Dirigo;* Charmian London miscarries

1913
John Barleycorn, The Valley of the Moon, and *The Abysmal Brute* are published

1914
Travels as a reporter to Mexico

1915
Visits Hawaii for the last time; *The Scarlet Plague* and *The Star Rover* are published

1916
Dies November 22 at Beauty Ranch

FURTHER READING

BOOKS BY JACK LONDON

The first editions of London's published books are listed here in chronological order. A number of these works have been republished and now exist in multiple editions, some of them recent. Several recent collections of London's short stories and letters are also included.

The Son of the Wolf. Boston: Houghton Mifflin, 1900. (short stories)

The God of His Fathers. New York: McClure, Phillips, 1901. (short stories)

Children of the Frost. New York: Macmillan, 1902. (short stories)

The Cruise of the Dazzler. New York: Century, 1902. (children's fiction)

A Daughter of the Snows. Philadelphia: J. B. Lippincott, 1902. (novel)

The Call of the Wild. New York: Macmillan, 1903. (novel)

The Kempton-Wace Letters. New York: Macmillan, 1903. With Anna Strunsky. (novel in letter form)

The People of the Abyss. New York: Macmillan, 1903. (social criticism)

The Faith of Men. New York: Macmillan, 1904. (short stories)

The Sea-Wolf. New York: Macmillan, 1904. (novel)

The Game. New York: Macmillan, 1905. (novel)

Tales of the Fish Patrol. New York: Macmillan, 1905. (children's fiction)

War of the Classes. New York: Macmillan, 1905. (essays)

Moon-Face and Other Stories. New York: Macmillan, 1906. (short stories)

Scorn of Woman. New York: Macmillan, 1906. (play)

White Fang. New York: Macmillan, 1906. (novel)

Before Adam. New York: Macmillan, 1907. (novel)

Love of Life and Other Stories. New York: Macmillan, 1907. (short stories)

The Road. New York: Macmillan, 1907. (essays)

The Iron Heel. New York: Macmillan, 1908. (novel)

Martin Eden. New York: Macmillan, 1909. (novel)

Burning Daylight. New York: Macmillan, 1910. (novel)

Lost Face. New York: Macmillan, 1910. (short stories)

Revolution and Other Essays. New York: Macmillan, 1910. (essays)

Theft: A Play in Four Acts. New York: Macmillan, 1910. (play)

Adventure. New York: Macmillan, 1911. (novel)

The Cruise of the Snark. New York: Macmillan, 1911. (essays)

South Sea Tales. New York: Macmillan, 1911. (short stories)

When God Laughs and Other Stories. New York: Macmillan, 1911. (short stories)

The House of Pride and Other Tales of Hawaii. New York: Macmillan, 1912. (short stories)

Smoke Bellew. New York: Century, 1912. (novel)

A Son of the Sun. Garden City, N.Y.: Doubleday, 1912. (short stories)

The Abysmal Brute. New York: Century, 1913. (novel)

John Barleycorn. New York: Century, 1913. (social criticism)

The Night-Born. New York: Century, 1913. (short stories)

The Valley of the Moon. New York: Macmillan, 1913. (novel)

The Mutiny of the Elsinore. New York: Macmillan, 1914. (novel)

The Strength of the Strong. New York: Macmillan, 1914. (short stories)

The Scarlet Plague. New York: Macmillan, 1915. (novel)

The Star Rover. New York: Macmillan, 1915. (novel)

The Acorn-Planter: A California Forest Play. New York: Macmillan, 1916. (play)

The Little Lady of the Big House. New York: Macmillan, 1916. (novel)

The Turtles of Tasman. New York: Macmillan, 1916. (short stories)

The Human Drift. New York: Macmillan, 1917. (essays)

Jerry of the Islands. New York: Macmillan, 1917. (novel)

Michael, Brother of Jerry. New York: Macmillan, 1917. (novel)

On the Makaloa Mat. New York: Macmillan, 1918. (short stories)

The Red One. New York: Macmillan, 1918. (short stories)

Hearts of Three. New York: Macmillan, 1920. (novel based on a screenplay)

Dutch Courage and Other Stories. New York: Macmillan, 1922. (short stories)

The Assassination Bureau, Ltd. New York: McGraw-Hill, 1963. Completed by Robert L. Fish. (novel)

The Letters of Jack London. Stanford, Calif.: Stanford University Press, 1988. Three volumes.

The Complete Short Stories of Jack London. Stanford, Calif.: Stanford University Press, 1993. Three volumes.

The Science Fiction Stories of Jack London. New York: Citadel Press, 1993.

The Portable Jack London. New York: Penguin, 1994.

The Jack London Reader. Philadelphia: Running Press, 1999.

Books about Jack London

Day, A. Grove. *Jack London in the South Seas.* New York: Four Winds, 1971.

Dyer, Daniel. *Jack London: A Biography.* New York: Scholastic, 1997.

Kershaw, Alex. *Jack London: A Life.* New York: St. Martin's, 1997.

Kingman, Russ. *Jack London: A Definitive Chronology.* Middletown, Calif.: David Rejl, 1992.

———. *A Pictorial Life of Jack London*. New York: Crown, 1979.

Labor, Earle, and Jeanne C. Reesman. *Jack London,* revised ed. New York: Twayne, 1994.

Lisandrelli, Elaine. *Jack London: A Writer's Adventurous Life*. Springfield, N.J.: Enslow, 1999.

London, Joan. *Jack London and His Daughters*. Berkeley, Calif.: Heyday, 1990.

Sinclair, Andrew. *Jack: A Biography of Jack London*. New York: Harper & Row, 1977.

Schroeder, Alan. *Jack London*. New York: Chelsea House, 1992.

Stasz, Clarice. *American Dreamers: Charmian and Jack London*. New York: St. Martin's, 1988.

Stone, Irving. *Sailor on Horseback: The Biography of Jack London*. Cambridge, Mass.: Houghton Mifflin, 1938.

Walker, Dale L., and Jeanne C. Reesman, editors. *No Mentor but Myself: Jack London on Writers and Writing*. Stanford, Calif.: Stanford University Press, 1999.

Williams, Tony. *Jack London: The Movies*. Middletown, Calif.: David Rejl, 1992.

Zamen, Mark. *Standing Room Only: Jack London's Controversial Career as a Public Speaker*. New York: Peter Lang, 1990.

Parks and Historic Sites

Jack London State Historical Park
2400 Jack London Ranch Road
Glen Ellen, CA 95442
(707) 938-5216
www.parks.sonoma.net/JLPark.html

Part of London's ranch has been made into this state park, near Glen Ellen. Jack London's grave is there, as are the ruins of Wolf House. Visitors can also tour some of the farm structures, including the "Pig Palace," and the museum that now occupies the House of Happy Walls, built by Charmian London after Jack's death. It houses their collections and other mementos of their life together and of Jack's working life.

Oakland Public Library
125 14th Street, 2nd floor
Oakland, CA 94612
(510) 238-3222
www.oaklandlibrary.org

The Oakland History Room in London's beloved Oakland Public Library contains various editions of his books as well as many photographs and articles relating to his life and career.

Jack London Square
Oakland, CA
(510) 814-6000
www.jacklondonsquare.com

Jack London Square, a shopping complex near the Oakland waterfront, includes the Jack London Museum and Bookstore, a replica of London's Henderson Creek cabin made in part of material from the original cabin (an identical replica of the cabin also stands in Dawson City, in the Yukon). Heinold's First and Last Chance Saloon, London's favorite bar in Oakland, is still in operation and its exterior has changed little since London's time.

Klondike Gold Rush National Historic Park
Second and Broadway
Skagway, AK 99840
(907) 983-9224
www.nps.gov/klgo/

This national park in Alaska celebrates the Klondike gold rush of 1897–98 with 15 restored buildings in the Skagway Historic District. The park also administers the Chilkoot Trail and a small portion of the White Pass Trail. Included in the park is a portion of the Dyea Townsite at the foot of the Chilkoot Trail.

Manuscript Collections

The Huntington Library in San Marino, California, houses the world's largest collection of documents connected with London's life and work. Other notable collections of London material are at the Bancroft Library of the University of California at Berkeley, the Merrill Library of Utah State University, the Department of Special Collections at the University of California at Los Angeles, and the California Historical Society. Except for special exhibitions, these collections are accessible only to scholars.

INDEX

References to illustrations and their captions are indicated by page numbers in *italics*.

Acknowledgments

Anyone who writes about Jack London must acknowledge an enormous debt to the multitude of scholars and researchers who have studied and written about London and his work. Among the most important publications on London—and the ones most helpful and inspiring to me—are those of Earle Labor, the leading modern London scholar, and the late Russ Kingman, who spent years researching and documenting London's adventurous life, taking special care to collect information from many people who had known Jack.

My own research was greatly aided by Gregory W. Hayes, state park ranger at Jack London State Historic Park, who provided insights into London's life at Beauty Ranch and recounted the stories behind many of the London possessions displayed in the House of Happy Walls; and by William Sturm, the knowledgeable librarian of the Oakland History Room at the Oakland Public Library, who pointed the way to scores of illuminating photographs and articles.

Picture Credits

(London, Jack-POR 37, 3-3 Call#, London, Jack-POR 4, London, Jack-POR 42, C-H 59 box 4 folder 12) Courtesy of the Bancroft Library/University of California, Berkeley, 2, 39, 84, 95, 108; Huntington Library, 25, 73,105; (LC-USZC4-3280, LC-USZ62-9360, LC-USZ62-112835, AP2.B6, NYWTS-4/18-19,1906) Library of Congress 14, 34, 53, 61, 81; Oakland Public Library cover, 6, 12, 16, 18, 23, 28, 46, 55, 64, 68, 69, 71, 76, 86, 92, 102; University of Utah Special Collections 89; MSCUA, University of Washington Libraries—Hegg 96, 53.

Text Credits

p. 24: From Jack London, *John Barleycorn,* (New York: Century, 1913), 61–62

p. 40: From Jack London, "Hoboes that Pass in the Night," *The Road,* 1907, online edition from University of California at Berkeley Digital Library, http://sunsite.berkeley.edu/London/Writings/The Road/hoboes.html

p. 56: From *Jack London Reports,* ed. King Hendricks and Irving Shepard (Garden City, N.Y.: Doubleday, 1970) 321–25

p. 79: From Jack London, *Novels and Social Writings,* (New York: Viking, 1982) 1153–60

p. 100: From Jack London, Chapter 1, *The Star Rover,* 1915, online edition from University of California at Berkeley Digital Library, http://sunsite.berkeley.edu/London/Writings/StarRover/chapter1.html

Rebecca Stefoff is the author of many nonfiction books for young adults, including *Charles Darwin and the Evolution Revolution* and the three-volume series *Extraordinary Explorers* both published by Oxford University Press. Her previous literary biographies include *Herman Melville* (Messner, 1994). Stefoff has also written extensively about U.S. history, especially the exploration and settling of the West. She lives in Portland, Oregon.

Stefoff, Rebecca.

Jack London.

DATE			